Judy —
Here's to your story!
[signature]

The People Project

Your Guide for Changing Behavior and
Growing Your Influence as a Leader

Steve Laswell

Next Level Executive Coaching, LLC

Published by Next Level Executive Coaching, LLC
www.nextlevelexecutivecoaching.com

Second printing, February 2012

Printed in the United States of America
Edited by LeAnn H. Gerst
Cover designed by Melinda H. Prescott

ISBN: 978-0615497297

Visit the author at **www.NextLevelExecutiveCoaching.com**

IMPORTANT NOTE

The names of coaching clients discussed in this book have been changed out of respect for their privacy.

❧In Their Own Words❧

"A rare and insightful blend of real-life experiences and practical advice, it is my privilege to recommend this book. Exciting and well written, *The People Project*, is a must read for anyone wanting to better understand their personal style and core motive. As a trusted colleague, Steve Laswell is one of the few executive coaches I know I can recommend to clients with complete confidence."

> – **Teri Aulph**, Teri Aulph Consulting, LLC, www.teriaulph.com
> Author of 'Experience Job Satisfaction

"During my coaching experience, Steve helped me to discover the power of open-ended questions. I used to just ask "why" and that was a barrier to my progress. Now I keep a sticky note on my desk at work to remind me to ask who, what, when, where and how – what a simple and highly effective concept."
> – **Sarah Phelps**, Human Resource Advisor

"Anytime my friend, Steve Laswell, talks about leadership, you need to listen. Anytime he talks about people, you should also listen carefully. But when Steve discusses leadership and how to influence people to change their behavior, you need to not only listen but you need to read and apply what he has to say! I look forward to seeing how "The People Project" influences others toward becoming who they were made to be!"

> – **Casey Cariker**, Lead Pastor, Rejoice Church

"Steve Laswell puts fascinating real-life experience into *The People Project*. His stories offer rare insight into the work of a top-level executive coach. *The People Project* is the kind of book you want to spend time with: Read a little, walk away and think about it, try things out and then come back for more."
> —**Karl Corbett**, Managing Partner, Sherpa Coaching

"A listener and encourager — that's what comes to mind when I think of Steve Laswell. I met Steve in the late '90's while going through a difficult time. He listened and asked the hard questions. Through the years, he has encouraged and challenged me to seek new paths and dream new dreams. I'm grateful for his influence on my life as a leader and mentor. Now, in *The People Project*, you will enjoy the stories, insights and yes, questions designed to accelerate your personal development."

– **Allison Hunsaker**, Principal, Vena Productions

"The People Project is a fascinating book! Antoine de Saint-Exupery, the French writer, said that, "A designer knows he has arrived at perfection not when there is no longer anything to add, but when there is no longer anything to take away." Such is the elegance of *The People Project*. It is simple, though not simplistic. Powerful, yet without needless complexity. And like all good designs, it is timeless.

I have been privileged to call Steve my friend for many years now, and in my experience, he has an incredible talent for identifying the most important thing – that singular thing that is standing between an individual and the attainment of his or her potential. In *The People Project*, he shares invaluable insight into how *you* can find that barrier, that one hurdle that is standing between you and the victory that might otherwise elude you.

In this book, you will also readily see Steve's love for people, a love refined by many years of practice. This book comes directly from his own journey, and I promise you that it will make your journey far more enjoyable."

– **Kelly S. Riggs**, President & Founder, Vmax Performance Group

❧Dedication❦

To you,
as you accept the call to leadership
and take the path of personal growth,
I dedicate **The People Project** to you.

❧Acknowledgments❧

It takes a great deal of support to experience personal growth and make the short journey of life count. In this regard, I am blessed and grateful for the many people who have touched my life. In like manner, this book is a collaborative effort.

My parents, **Jim and Vivian Laswell**, provided a significant foundation for a character-based life and work ethic. Not just by example, but through learned leadership of my life with paper routes and lawn services as a kid. Moreover, they provided my spiritual heritage and allowed me to discover the place of faith in life, which guides how I do life to this very day.

To my best friend, parenting partner, #1 fan, and wife of over 35 years. Thank you, **Rita**, for making it possible to dream the dream and pursue my passion. I could not have done this without your support, given freely and in so many ways. You love with unconditional love and are an amazing woman.

How significant to have our three daughters **Stephanie, Monica, and Melanie**, and their husbands **Jeffrey, Severiano, and Brian**, cheering me on.

There are **key players** specific to the launch of Next Level Executive Coaching, LLC. Each one of you played your unique role. Without your input my executive coaching practice would not be thriving today. Be assured, I know the impact of your influence; your insight, support, belief in me, and help has been a gift. Thank you for that lunch, breakfast, or coffee, that email or phone call that came at just the right time.

Then, there are all of you who listened and allowed me to process the years of transition. You were there as I found the words to describe the dream; you helped make this a reality. Thank you for your part in the Story, The People Project, and Next Level Executive Coaching, LLC.

To **my** coaching clients: **thank you** for showing up authentically. Your pursuit of personal growth is amazing. You signed up for the Next Level Journey, challenged the box, and found your spacious place of freedom. Congratulations! You did the work. You opened up to truth and your reward was greater freedom and personal success as men and women, leaders, and emerging leaders. You created space to reflect on truth delivered through the Story. Thank you for the privilege of supporting you on your leadership journey.

To Jesus Christ, my Savior, the giver of all things good and life eternal . . . Thank You!

Steve Laswell
June 2011

❧Contents❧

Harmony: The New Work-Life Balance

Personal Growth: The Journey of a Lifetime

Conclusion

About the Author

Sources

∿Foreword∿

All of us want to succeed in business and life. Unfortunately, too few people understand success or how to get it. Success is a self-fulfilling prophecy. You get to decide where the target is and when you have reached it. In this book, Steve Laswell will share with you how to get from where you are to where you want to be. These are the two key elements of success.

I am reminded of the store map displays in shopping malls. In various places throughout the mall, you will find a diagram showing the location of each store or shop within the building. There are two critical elements you must know in order to use the map. You must know where you are and where you want to go.

By virtue of the fact that you are holding this book in your hands, I assume that there are things you want to achieve in life and places you want to go. As you hold the vision of success in your mind, Steve will guide you toward your goal through five key principles.

1. **Communication: The Key to Connecting.** None of us succeed on our own. We have to have the creativity and effort of talented people around us, and unless you can communicate with them, you cannot succeed.
2. **People Skills: The Business of Business is People.** All of us are in the people business. We want to work with and do business with people we like and understand and people who we feel like and care about us.
3. **Leadership: Growing Your Personal Influence.** You cannot motivate or push people to success. You must lead them.
4. **Harmony: The New Work-Life Balance.** We are all faced with too many tasks and not enough hours in the day.

If we're not careful, we end up making other people's priorities our own while ignoring the people and things that mean the most to us.

5.   **Personal Growth: The Journey of a Lifetime.** When we understand that success is planted on the inside and manifests itself on the outside, we begin to realize that the knowledge we gain and the wisdom we apply are the keys to our success. Gathering this knowledge and wisdom is an investment we make in our future and in our success.

I met Steve Laswell in conjunction with a project we did together to assist people who had lost their jobs. Steve has a real compassion for people facing challenges and a passion to help them succeed. Through the event, I met a number of people who, after getting over the shock of losing their job, realized that unemployment had offered them the opportunity to re-evaluate where they were and where they wanted to be. The event for unemployed people, which was Steve's brainchild, was about turning lemons into lemonade. While I think it's a great thing to reassess where you are and where you want to be, don't wait until you're unemployed or face a business crisis before you engage in the process.

We all had dreams and goals when we were teenagers or young adults. There were things we wanted to be, do, have, create, and give away. In our youth, we were convinced that we could change the world, but then somewhere between there and here, we may have gotten so busy making a living that we forgot to create a life.

I hope you will take Steve's words and lessons as a wakeup call to recalibrate where you're going and how you're going to get there.

I wish you happy reading and great success.

Jim Stovall
Author of *The Ultimate Gift* and *Ultimate Productivity*

Introduction

࿐Introduction࿐

The conversation shifted from reconnecting with one of my executive coaching clients to an opportunity when the Fortune 500 VP said, "I have a project for you." He continued to tell me about an executive manager he wanted me to coach.

As I hung up, the word "project" continued to roll around in my mind. A "project." *Is that what people are?* The more I thought it over the more I hoped Jack was referring to the coaching engagement, not the coaching client.

The People Project is designed to *accelerate* your personal development as a both a person and a leader.

By definition, a project is a planned undertaking. **The People Project** is your guide to leadership development. Leadership involves engaging and expanding as a person. The basic skill of leadership is tied to your ability to lead, guide, direct, and influence people. The keyword is **influence.** The essence of leadership is to accomplish something; leadership is influencing people to accomplish a task.

> *"The very essence of leadership is its purpose. And the purpose of leadership is to accomplish a task. That is what leadership does—and what it does is more important than what it is or how it works."*
>
> *– Colonel Dandridge M. Malone*

To enlarge your personal influence requires leading your life.

"Leadership is understanding people and involving them to help you do a job. That takes all of the good characteristics, like integrity, dedication of purpose, selflessness, knowledge, skill, implacability, as well as determination not to accept failure."

– Admiral Arleigh A. Burke

Leadership involves influence; development involves change. While expanding your personal influence with others includes your own personal growth, development includes helping others in *like manner.* Development speaks to the process of changing and becoming stronger as well as *helping others* become more successful, stronger, or advanced.

Leadership development is **engaging** in the *process of change* while **expanding** your *personal influence.*

Henry Kissinger is quoted to have said, *"The task of the leader is to get his people from where they are to where they have not been."* This is the positive ramification of a leader's development.

By design, the chapters in this book are quick reads gathered in five categories for easy reference. You will find a few questions to support deeper reflection on the subject so that you can engage in the process of change.

I hope **The People Project** becomes a resource to accelerate your leadership development and that of the lives around you in your workplace, your home, and your community.

"If your actions inspire others to dream more, learn more, do more and become more, you are a leader."

– John Quincy Adams

Communication

The Key to Connecting

1

The Quill Pig

Mike was an emerging leader. His personal development needs included his ability to communicate—especially with the owner of the company.

As Mike shared his story, I could see how his **fear of confrontation** made it difficult to effectively communicate with his boss.

Our conversation went something like this...

> "Mike, how do you like being told what to do? When you are given an assignment, you know what to do *and* how to proceed. How does being told what to do affect you?"
> "I don't like it," he replied.
> "Why is that?"
> "I like to be left alone to do my job; trust me and let me do it."
> I pressed on, "How does it make you feel when someone tells you what to do?"
> After some hesitation he found his words, "I don't like it and find myself resisting...I don't feel trusted or respected."

When was the last time you enjoyed being **told** what to do?

Consider communication and the lovable porcupine. National Geographic helps us understand this animal's unique qualities (emphasis added):

"The porcupine is the **prickliest** of rodents, though its Latin name means "quill pig." There are about two dozen porcupine species, and all boast a coat of needle-like quills to give predators a **sharp reminder** that this animal is no easy meal. Some quills, like those of Africa's crested porcupine, are nearly a foot (30 cm) long.

Porcupines have soft hair, but on their back, sides, and tail it is usually mixed with sharp quills. These quills typically lie flat until a porcupine is **threatened**, then leap to attention as a **persuasive deterrent**. Porcupines cannot shoot them at predators as once thought, but the quills do **detach easily** when touched.

Many animals come away from a porcupine encounter with quills protruding from their own snouts or bodies. Quills have sharp tips and overlapping scales or barbs that make them **difficult to remove** once they are stuck in another animal's skin. Porcupines grow new quills to replace the ones they lose."

How many people have a pet porcupine that you know? How close do you want to be to this rodent?

Notice the keywords from the description of the Quill Pig. Here's how I connect them to **telling** in communication:

- **Prickly:** An uncomfortable, irritating, defensive exchange.

- **Sharp Reminder:** What do you think "tellers" want others to remember? Why the intensity?

- **Threatened:** What fear drives the need to "tell"?

- **Persuasive Deterrent:** What is limited by a "telling" style of communication?

- **Detach Easily:** Why is it "easier" to tell?

- **Difficult to Remove:** "Sticks and stones may break my bones, but words cannot harm me." Really?

Do you want to be known as a **Quill Pig**?

At a relationship level, "telling" often shuts dialog down; effective leaders avoid this communication style.

Telling Pushes People Away

Imagine a ball carrier in football. His goal is the end zone. As he runs toward defenders, their goal is to tackle him. With an outstretched arm, the ball carrier pushes his hand onto his would-be tackler to take him out of the action. The "stiff arm" is designed to push the other player out of the way.

This is just another example of how telling hinders communication.

The Solution: Ask More . . .

Having established the imagery of "telling" with Mike, we moved on to the alternative.

> "Mike, when someone you respect asks for your input, your opinion, your thoughts on a topic, how do you feel?"
> "Oh, it's great. I feel honored, respected; appreciated, valued, trusted...it's totally different."

Yes, it is "totally different" when we ask open-ended questions. That's because open-ended questions invite participation.

- Asking encourages an exchange of *ideas through dialogue and discussion.*

- Asking *sends a message* of value, respect, and honor.

- Asking *shows* a level of trust and appreciation.

- Asking *flows* from a place of freedom.
- Asking *indicates a released* need to control.

Whereas **telling** "pushes people away," **asking** "invites them to stay."

Teach When You Can

Of course, there is a time to impart knowledge to someone, to provide direction, to advocate a certain way or even the way something must be done. When these moments arise, go for it. Be a great teacher.

The Quill Pig mantra:

Ask More, Tell Less, Teach When You Can

Through our discussion, Mike discovered that asking questions is *not* confrontational; in fact, it actually demonstrated honor, respect, and appreciation—even for his boss.

Your Personal Reflection

- ❖ What's your *default* communication style?

- ❖ What do you think about the mantra "**Ask MORE, Tell LESS, Teach When You Can**"?

- ❖ In what areas of your life can you tell less and ask more?

2

The Power of a Question

Recently, one of my clients requested coaching for her employees.

Providing coaching, whether through a 1on1 session or to a group is always exciting. I knew this manager's decision to provide coaching for her staff would not only have a positive effect on her team, but the business as well.

After exploring needs and calendars, we scheduled their first Employee Leadership Development session.

Later that evening, as my wife Rita and I were walking, she celebrated with me. She then asked an interesting question. "How does the Employee Leadership Development compare to your 1on1 Executive Coaching and Next Level TEAM Coaching?"

Her open-ended question immediately caused me to stop and think.

My wife's question sent me on a journey. Over the next couple of days my answer came, along with a greater clarity and focus to my coaching practice.

That's what a well-framed question does. It invites us to stop and think. And that's good.

The open-ended question is a request for information and is designed to help us stop and explore for truth. Here's why . . .

1. Slow down

Questions **s l o w   t h i n g s   d o w n**, offering protection from knee-jerk reactions.

Have you noticed how quickly you can answer a "yes/no" question? However, an open-ended question (those starting with *who, what, how, when, where, or why*) can interrupt an emotionally charged conversation and help get the conversation back on track.

2. Show respect

How do you feel when "the boss" seeks your input? An authentic question, especially in the midst of problem solving or decision making, demonstrates respect and trust. A well-framed, open-ended question is helpful and powerful.

3. Create space

To discover truth we need space—a time and place to think.

Creating space is the disciplined use of time, place, and resources for reflection on the truth found in the story.

We must slow the pace to create the space required to experience personal development. If we don't, we can easily be overtaken by today's time conspiracy—a subversive plot to keep us so busy we don't have the time or a place for thinking, consideration, or consistent reflection.

Why the pursuit of truth in the story? Because truth liberates.

Truth sheds light and opens our minds to possibilities—even when it **hurts**.

What happens if you run from the truth (reality/facts)? You wind up hindering your growth and potential, and ultimately running from your destiny and future success.

What is the best predictor of future success? Here's my thought:

> *The Best Predictor of Future Success is the ability and willingness to learn and change achieved through consistent reflection on truth found in the story.*

Questions help us give careful thought to reality. The facts in the story (when examined) become feedback. Truth allows us to choose to change unproductive behavior, enlarge our influence (leadership), achieve success, and make a difference in the world.

So remember: open-ended questions can help you **slow down** an emotionally charged conversation, **demonstrate respect**, and **create space** to discover solutions.

My wife Rita's question was very powerful, as it helped shape an additional coaching service: the power of a question.

Your Personal Reflection

- ❖ How effective are you in using questions?

- ❖ How does a question help?

- ❖ How much space do you have in your daily life for reflection?

☙3☙

Ask More, Tell Less

What happens when you lead with a well-framed question?

Consider your response if I was coaching you and said:

> "Look, **you** must stop telling people what to do; **I need you** to start asking more questions. **I want you** to use open-ended questions, not yes/no questions. **You** will not motivate people by telling them what to do. So make sure to do it this way."

How would you feel?

If you're like most people, you'd take offense. As a result, you might defend yourself or shut down all together. My guess is I'd probably never see you again after our session. Why do you think that is?

The Framing of a Great Question

An open-ended question involves the use of *who, what, when, where, how*, and sometimes *why* (if you're careful with tone of voice).

For example, what is the effect if you ask, *"What are your thoughts on this plan?"* instead of *"Do you like this plan?"*

A closed-question is answered with "yes" or "no" and stops the conversation. A well-framed question *invites* dialog and encourages input.

There is a relationship benefit associated with well-framed questions. Asking more and telling less when communicating with those you lead helps instill:

- **Honor**: When you seek their input, they feel respected and valued.

- **Objectivity**: A well-timed question slows the conversation down in a positive way.

- **Cooperation**: Support and willingness to comply are more likely to be given.

- **Performance**: Where there is honor, objectivity, and cooperation, the effectiveness in response improves.

Just remember the mantra: **Ask More, Tell Less, Teach When You Can.**

Your Personal Reflection

- ❖ What is the impact of a well-framed question on the communication experience?

- ❖ What is the impact of a well-framed question on the person?

- ❖ When someone you respect asks you an open-ended question, how does it make you feel?

Gifted Hands

Carol is a Fortune 500 Manager and an **emerging leader**. Her name comes up as succession planning is discussed by her VP. She has distinguished herself over the past nine years and is quite grateful for the opportunities. She brags on her team as some of the brightest. She enjoys her work. She is a "keeper."

Carol's aspirations are significant; *succession planning* is on **her mind**, too. She intends to replace her VP in a few years and is looking at her next level beyond that. Carol believes in herself and her abilities.

She is also aware that something is getting in her way. Her story is a classic illustration of what Marshall Goldsmith points out in his book, *What Got you **Here** Won't Get You **There***. Carol understands this principle; however, she was seeking support for the additional personal growth and professional development required to "get there."

Benjamin S. Carson, M.D., is one of the world's foremost pediatric neurosurgeons. Born in Detroit to a single mother in a working-class neighborhood, he is Professor and Chief of Pediatric Neurosurgery at Johns Hopkins University Medical School.

I appreciate what he writes in his autobiography, Gifted Hands, about developing our potential (emphasis added):

> "In any career, whether it's that of a TV repairman, a musician, a secretary - or a surgeon - an individual must

believe in himself and in his abilities. To do his best, one needs a confidence that says, "I can do anything, and if I can't do it, *I know how to get help*.""

When Carol and I started her executive coaching engagement, she was solid in work intensity, drive, ambition, determination, and the technical aspects of her work. Yet, there was something holding her back. It's true, what got her where she is today will not get her where she wants to be tomorrow. But the good news is that she *understood how to receive help* and *embrace objective support* for her personal growth.

Carol is now connecting the dots between her recent performance feedback, the person she is, and her business behavior. She is accepting help, making changes, and making the most of today while on her way to "getting there."

Your Personal Reflection

- ❖ What are you trying to accomplish that you really can't do alone?

- ❖ What are *your* thoughts on asking for help? Do you see it as a sign of weakness? Or is it only about making something easier, more likely, or better?

- ❖ How do you feel about securing support for your personal growth?

❧5❧

What's Got You Jumping?

I was in Cincinnati for the annual Sherpa Coaching Conference as part of my re-certification. The group was large enough and the schedule full enough that it was impossible to connect with everyone. I only knew a few people.

After the conference, I grabbed a bite to eat at the airport with a coaching colleague from Dallas. As we finished our meal, another executive coach entered the restaurant. I had observed her over the past few days, but an assumption kept me from connecting. It wasn't until that "last chance to connect conversation" that I discovered a great person.

Her story was amazing. She was an emergency room doctor, just certified and transitioning from medicine to executive coaching.

Nearly a year later, I reached out to her and we re-connected by phone. The longer our conversation, the more we shared in our approach to coaching. It was a great human connection.

In reflecting on the incident, I felt the effect of making *assumptions*.

How do assumptions get us in trouble?

Assumptions are made when you think you know something and accept it as true without verifying it. Assumptions show up when we take something for granted *without* proof.

The primary characteristic of an assumption is the *lack of verification* or proof.

What is the effect of making an assumption?

1. **Deception:** You believe something to be true that is not.
2. **Bondage:** You lose an opportunity to make a decision based on truth.

On the other hand, how does judgment help us make wise decisions?

Judgment has to do with forming an opinion ***after*** consideration, observation, or the pursuit of truth. This leadership ability to form a sound opinion and make sound decisions is significantly different than making assumptions.

We know that judgment can refer to a decision handed down by a court of law or a judge. In this case, a decision is reached after considerable examination of the facts.

What is the effect of exercising judgment?

1. **Discernment:** You form a sound opinion and make better decisions.
2. **Freedom:** You are able to act and live intentionally, less reactive.

What does it take to exercise judgment over making assumptions?

You must **create space**. By that I mean you must make time to pursue the truth of The Story. Making assumptions is a **limiting behavior** driven by first impressions, jumping to conclusions, and a closed thought process. Exercising judgment is a **success-oriented behavior** driven by self-awareness, reflection, and open mindedness.

To manage the assumption trap, you must be able to ask open-ended questions. This requires challenging your assumption by asking:

- Why do I believe this?
- How do I know this to be true?
- What am I basing my conclusion on?
- How are my filters impacting my ability to see this person? Situation?

Remember: the business of life is people. A lot of people problems and lost opportunities are tied to the *limiting behavior* of making assumptions and jumping to conclusions.

Slow it down. Check your thinking. Ask questions. The reward is worth the effort.

If it had not been for my "second chance," I would have lost the opportunity to connect with a dynamic individual. When I finally took the time to connect with her, I received affirmation and encouragement on my presentation at the conference. To think, I almost lost that gift because of a limiting behavior—making an assumption.

Your Personal Reflection

- ❖ What assumptions do you make about others?

- ❖ What is that costing you?

- ❖ Think of a recent assumption you made about another person. How might your perception have changed had you asked questions?

People Skills

The Business of Business is People

❧6❧

Her Gentle Giant

Room 224 of St. Francis Hospital was right across from the nurse's station. The door was open; I went in but did not recognize the man I came to see.

No one was in the room; the patient's name was not posted on the white board with the other erasable bits of information. So, I stepped across the hall to check with the nurse, just to be sure I had the right room. I did; it was John.

When I spoke to John I didn't get much of a response other than slowly turning his head to look in my direction. Was he seeing me? I wasn't sure.

Shortly thereafter, his nurse, Teresa, stepped in; confident and bold like you would expect from someone in charge. She went to the other side of John's bed, speaking to me, then to John, then back to me. John responded to Teresa. She spoke up; I must have been too soft spoken.

John was doing a bit better today; a difficult surgery.

As Teresa was leaving, she said, "I think of him as a Gentle Giant; was he?"

It was apparent that John was a tall man; he filled the bed from one end to the other. I mumbled something to indicate my agreement. But I really didn't know John; he was just someone that attended my church and was now home-bound; I simply volunteered to check in on him.

"Yes, I just picture him as my gentle giant," she repeated as she slipped out of the room.

There I remained at silent John's bedside; questions filled my mind: What was John like when he was a boy...a young man? What was his line of work? Who is this man that now lies here sedated with morphine to manage the pain? What is his legacy? Will he ever walk again? How are his wife and family doing?

My steps were slow as I left John's room and walked down the hall, temporarily lost in my thoughts.

Life happens quickly.

Add to this experience my recent four-day weekend. Rita and I went to Edmond to grand-parent four of our grandchildren. Again, I'm aware of how quickly life happens. It wasn't long ago that our oldest daughter Stephanie was our granddaughter's age.

When was the last time you noticed **life happens quickly**?

Time is a limited resource. There is a mysterious restriction placed on how much time you are given in this life.

Life happens quickly *and* **the business of life is people**; relationships, connecting, re-connecting, partnering, and our friendships.

Life happens quickly, the business of life is people, *and* **the business of business is people**.

Peter Bregman speaks, writes, and consults on leadership. In his recent Harvard Business Review post, *Why Friends Matter at Work and in Life,* he writes about his mother-in-law, Susan.

> "Susan was, quite simply, a really good friend. Which is an art. To be a good friend, you have to give of yourself, but not so much that you lose yourself. You need to know what you want and pursue it, while helping others achieve what they want. You need to have personality while making room for, and supporting, other people's personalities. You need to care about, and even love, people you might disagree with. You need to be willing to give at least as much, if not more, than you take."

I wasn't sure when or how John would leave Room 224. But if I could have asked him, I'm certain he would have affirmed that life happens quickly.

Come to think of it, I don't know how much time I have. But I do know life happens quickly, that the business of life is people, and the business of business is people.

Your Personal Reflection

- ❖ How well are you connecting with life?

- ❖ The business of business is people. How do you see work associates, customers, clients, employees?

- ❖ In what way has the fast pace of life kept you from connecting with the people of your business?

❧7❧

You Know My Name!

"You know my name!"

That was the response Jennifer, in accounting, received from a frontline employee. What did she do? All she did was respond to his request with the words, "Your name is Mark, right?"

Why did Mark give such an emotional response?

"You know my name!" reveals a lot to the discerning leader of people. What do you see or hear in his words?

Here are a few key words around engagement; not exhaustive, just a few simple thoughts about *Connecting, Respect, Value, and Giving Voice.*

1. Connecting

When it comes to employee engagement, we know it is not about the exchange of time for money. It is about connecting. Just as a connecting flight allows you to arrive at your destination, so does a good connection with the people in your organization.

Nature makes the **performance value** of connecting easy to understand. Consider the tomato plant and notice all the connections that allow it to create my favorite fruits.

In general, the plant uses its roots to extract water from the soil; its leaves absorb carbon dioxide from the air and energy from the sun.

The stem transports the water and nutrients, producing both oxygen AND the delicious tomato.

Remove any one of those connections and we can forget the desired and delicious outcome.

The ability to connect or join people together in a common cause—too often called a "soft" skill—is actually a **core** leadership skill. Your capacity to get along with people and connect them to one another as a "team" is more important than ever.

2. Respect

Beyond connecting, support of employee engagement can occur as we meet the human need for *respect*. In simplest terms, respect is *showing consideration and thoughtfulness to another person.*

A deep appreciation associated with admiration and deference toward someone is required for collaboration. To free an employee to give their best while withholding respect is unproductive. When a leader fails to earn the respect of others, loyalty and commitment will be missing.

This basic respect goes a long way in human relationships and allows us to get things done. When we redirect our focus from self to others and care about them, the performance will come.

3. Value

A rigid, bottom-line focus makes it is easy to lose sight of the person. Once a person begins to feel viewed like an object, disengagement is sure to follow. We **value a person** when we care enough to acknowledge their worth and importance as a human *person* more than their usefulness as a human *being.*

Quite often, part of my service to leaders is that of reminding. Jennifer's story prompts this friendly reminder, which comes from Gallup's research, originally released in **First, Break All the Rules** and then, **12: The Elements of Great Managing.** You may know about the concepts. It comes in the form of a question, which made the top 5 out of the list of 12 great managing elements:

> *"Does my supervisor, or someone at work, seem to care about me as a person?"*

Yes, the intent of Question 5 goes beyond just knowing an employees' name. People want to know: *Do you care about me...are you interested in my story...do you have concern beyond the job I do...do you care about my working conditions?*

Whether the new reality show *Undercover Boss* is all that it appears to be or not, I see one consistent message: these CEOs are **re*learning*** the **value** of their frontline people and the work they do.

4. Giving Voice

Our leadership influence is limited if our ability to connect, respect, and value others doesn't include *giving voice* to others. To evaluate how well you give voice to others consider how often you:

- Remain open to the ideas and opinions of others
- Finish other people's sentences
- Take credit for work others accomplished
- "Tell" others how to complete an assignment upon delegating it to them, beyond stating the desired outcome
- Listen to others

In answer to the question *"How can we help someone find his or her voice?"*, Stephen Covey responds (emphasis added:

"I think if you **care** about people genuinely, you **listen to** them and **observe** them; because *this is more than just hearing them speak*, it is observing them - observing where their excitement is, where their enthusiasm is; observing where you sense they have potential.

Sometimes it is very powerful just to say to them in sincerity, "I believe you have great potential in this area. I see real strengths in you that you may not see in yourself, and I would like to create an opportunity for you to use those strengths and to develop this potential. Would you be interested in that?""

These core concepts are really about how you, as a leader, *engage* your people.

What is the biggest problem a manager faces today?

During a *Gallup Management Journal* interview, Rodd Wagner, a principal at Gallup, and James K. Harter, Ph.D., chief scientist for Gallup's international workplace management practice, were asked, *"What is the biggest problem manager's face today?"* Here's what they had to say:

"There are actually two primary problems facing managers.

First is the idea that almost anyone can be a manager, when in fact, it requires certain talents and really ought to be viewed as a specialty. This view often puts the wrong people in management jobs and creates too little focus on improving the quality of managing.

Second is the contempt for what are sometimes *dismissively called the "soft skills" of working with people* compared with the "hard skills" of understanding numbers and processes. Great managers are incredibly perceptive about human nature. It's a rare and typically undervalued ability."

There is more to employee engagement than these four core people skills—connecting, respect, value, and giving voice. However, using these core skills to build relationships encourages high-performing teams.

Your Personal Reflection

- ❖ How well do you engage your people?

- ❖ How well do you *connect, respect, value, and give voice to* your employees? How effectively do your leaders engage employees *at all levels*?

- ❖ What core people skill have you identified as one to give attention to? How will you sharpen this skill?

≈8≈

The Cost of Disengagement

The act of breaking off an engagement to be married, canceling the wedding plans, and managing gifts received is not high on any engaged couple's list. Not only is it an expensive loss, with lost deposits and time, disengagement is emotionally painful.

According to Curt Coffman, Global Practice Leader for Q12 Management Consulting and coauthor of Gallup's best-selling book, *First, Break All the Rules,* a large portion of the work force is living with the emotionally painful process of disengagement:

> ". . . **55%** of all U.S. workers are **not engaged**, and **16%** are **actively disengaged**, then **71% of the Americans** who go to work every day aren't engaged in their role."

The reality is sobering—71% of today's employees live each day with the emotional pain of disengagement at work. That's the human capital bad news, but there is more to this story.

American businesses are operating at one third of their capacity. Think about that: what if only one third of a bank's branches opened each day? What if only one third of a manufacturing company's machines operated at capacity every day?

Levels of Engagement

As outlined in Gallup's review, an engaged leader faces three levels of employee engagement: **engaged**, **not engaged**, or **actively disengaged**.

The **"engaged"** employees are *builders*. They use their talents, develop productive relationships, and multiply their effectiveness through those relationships. They perform at consistently high levels. They drive innovation and move their organization forward.

The employees that are **"not engaged"** aren't necessarily negative or positive about their company. They basically *take a wait-and-see attitude* toward their job, their employer, and their coworkers. They hang back and don't commit themselves.

This brings us to the **"actively disengaged"** employees, otherwise known as the "CAVE dwellers." They're "**C**onsistently **A**gainst **V**irtually **E**verything." We've all worked with an actively disengaged employee who is not just unhappy at work; he *acts out that unhappiness*. Every day, actively disengaged employees *tear down* what their engaged coworkers are building.

As Kerry Sulkowicz's points out: ". . . if employees don't feel that their (boss) isn't the real McCoy on a human level, they won't respond very well. They react with distrust, disengagement, and even despair at the prospect of an automaton at the helm."

Fortunately, there is some good news, and that is this: where there is disengagement, there is also an *opportunity for growth*.

Returning to the analogy of our engaged couple, beyond their commitment level, what do we find? What must a couple have to move forward in a lifelong relationship?

To stay the course requires commitment *and* passion. For a couple, this intense emotion is the result of liking each other. They are "enthusiastic" about the each other. They are passionate about having found the "love of their life."

Staying engaged as an employee also requires commitment *and* passion. They must feel passionate about their work to remain committed to their job, their boss, and their company.

Even when you *are* an engaged leader, if your employees are not passionate about their role, it will be difficult for them to remain engaged and committed. Living life with purpose and passion while serving others is the key to a satisfying work life experience.

As a leader, it's up to you to take the first step towards closing the gap of disengagement. You can do so by living as an engaged leader and embracing the *opportunity for growth*.

Your Personal Reflection

❖ When it comes to levels of people engagement, how do you stack up against Gallop's statistics?

❖ How is employee disengagement costing you and your company?

❖ What would happen in your organization if it had an increase in *engaged* people?

༺9༻

The Keys to Engagement

Whether you lead a company, own your own business, manage a department, or work for someone else, employee engagement matters.

Reality check: employers & employees, leaders & teams, managers & staff—you're either in this together or you're not.

In light of the fact that the "or not" path is very expensive, it pays to give attention to this. Yes, there is a reduction of pain and an increase in profit with every percentage point increase of engaged people.

Quick Review: What do we know about people engagement in work?

- Chronic employee *disengagement* is very costly to business and people.
- Relationship concepts include:
    - ✓ **Connecting**
    - ✓ **Respecting**
    - ✓ **Valuing**
    - ✓ **Having Voice**
- Step One of engagement is in your court: how engaged are **you**?
- The 3 levels of employee engagement:
    1. "**Engaged**" – a *contributor*
    2. "**Not engaged**" – *a wait-and-see attitude*

3. The "**actively disengaged**" – *consistently against virtually everything*

- Disengagement is an *emotionally painful* way to work and live for everyone
- Gallup suggests **55%** of all U.S. workers are **not engaged** while another **16%** are **actively disengaged**
- There is some **good news**...the *opportunity for growth*
- **Commitment** and **passion** are basic to long-term employee engagement

What are the keys to engagement?

In the book *Closing the Engagement Gap*, Julie Gebauer and Don Lowman share Towers Perrin's groundbreaking research and knowledge around employee engagement. They draw on stories from CEOs, managers and employees from eight extraordinary organizations in technology, health care, retail, manufacturing, consumer goods, and entertainment.

Here are the five keys they suggest will unlock your employees' potential:

1. **Know Them.** Be as familiar with employees as you are with customers. Use that knowledge to shape workplace programs that win people's hearts and minds.
2. **Grow Them.** Challenge and develop the workforce. People want to learn and excel in their jobs, and they commit to companies that help them.
3. **Inspire Them.** Establish an emotional connection. When people's work has meaning, they are more inclined to do whatever it takes to ensure success.
4. **Involve Them.** Communicate clearly with employees, gather their input, and let them act. Knowledgeable, valued workers add more value.
5. **Reward Them.** Deliver a "deal" that is fair and meaningful. When people believe they are treated right and

appreciated, they give more of their time and creative energy.

Your Personal Reflection

- ❖ The above five keys are from an employer's perspective. As an employee, how can you re-position the five keys?

- ❖ How would you rate your experience with these five keys?

- ❖ How do you think you could "manage up" to close the gap?

ᔆ10ᔆ

The Beauty of Appreciation

Heather is a valuable employee of a beauty products company that does business internationally. We met for coffee to discuss a challenge she was having with work. Despite her company's overall mission to promote "harmony" between people by enhancing the way we live and interact with each other, Heather wasn't feeling the beauty of that harmony in her experience with her manager.

Over the past six years, Heather had developed herself from an entry-level employee to an individual with a strong work ethic. Perhaps that explained one of the reasons she was now an assistant manager.

As our java chat (coaching conversation over coffee) continued, she began to confide in me, so I asked, *"What is your challenge today?"* The bottom line answer: her growing disengagement at work.

In addition to Heather's positive career path with the company, she was consistently hitting performance goals. She was also identified as an emerging leader by the company's regional corporate leaders—an awesome achievement, indeed. So why then were we having this java chat? Why was she thinking about leaving?

Did she like what she was doing? Yes.

Was she a "good employee" making a difference; did she have highly valued character qualities? Yes.

Had her employer invested time and money in her personal growth and professional development? Yes.

Was she growing as a person, an assistant manager, a leader? Yes.

Did her company see an enlarged role in her future? Yes.

Then, why was she considering an exit strategy?

If you ask, "How much of a raise did she want?" you asked the wrong question.

Forward thinking leaders would ask:

- What can we do to hold on to this **valuable person** (employee)?
- How will we protect our **investment** in her training, experience, product knowledge, the personal development of this person, *and* all her customer relationships?
- What will it take to avoid the **high cost of turnover** (most agree it is 3 to 5 times an employee's salary; so this loss would have *hidden* costs of $100,000)?

Of note is that her salary was never mentioned, and neither was the substantial demand of her schedule.

As my frozen mocha coffee was all but gone and she answered my questions, the solution for keeping this emerging leader became quite clear: **appreciation**. Her manager was missing an important skill—the ability to communicate basic appreciation.

One simple behavior change—her manager showing some appreciation for a job well done, for going the extra mile, for making their store the top performer in the company—and

Heather would be on board. She would feel valued and give her best.

Now, how do you suppose her manager would respond if I were to ask, *"Do you appreciate Heather?"* Correct. She would probably say something along the lines of *"We love Heather, she's great."*

Here's the bottom line: *appreciation, by definition, only exists when it is* expressed. Appreciation is admiration, approval, or gratitude **expressed**.

Recent U.S. Department of Labor data shows that the number one reason people leave their job is that they do not feel appreciated. (And by the way, customer loyalty is also based on feeling appreciated.)

Unfortunately, the reality is that admiration, approval, and gratitude are left **un**expressed far too often; that's insane. The return on the investment in relationship building and performance is amazing.

What is the message when admiration, approval, or gratitude is not communicated? Have you noticed how most people, if left on their own, imagine the worst-case scenario? That means people will assume you disapprove of their performance or of them if you don't express some form of appreciation.

Let's keep it simple: appreciation must be shown to have an impact. That means you must let those around you know your thoughts, and you must demonstrate your approval, gratitude, or admiration for their contribution.

There are several ways to express appreciation. It doesn't always have to be a grand gesture. In fact, expressing appreciation can be quite easy. Here are a few suggestions:

1. **Be intentional;** notice others and their contributions.
2. **Seize the moment;** when you notice say something right then.
3. **Know your people;** know what matters to them (public vs. private praise, etc.).
4. **Leverage existing opportunities;** take time for a birthday lunch or coffee, celebrate their date of hire, etc.
5. **Brag on them to someone special;** send a note, an email, or make a brief phone call.

What will it cost the company if Heather leaves? At minimum, the **hidden costs** associated with turnover.

When you show appreciation for a person and their contribution, they'll be more likely to remain engaged and perform at a higher level.

Your Personal Reflection

❖ What's that performance boost worth to you?

❖ What's your plan for boosting the performance of your team?

❖ How well are you showing appreciation of others around you?

Leadership

Growing Your Personal Influence

⫷11⫸

Leadership: Gift or Game?

In hearing my friend, Jon Middendorf, speak in Oklahoma City, his message brought to light a great question: *"Is life a game or a gift?"* As I reflected on this question, I began to connect it to the life of a leader.

What happens when leadership becomes a game?

I was struck by the following information, which I found on Games Information Depot, regarding the rules for the board game Life.

> "The main thing that you need to know is that the game of Life has changed a lot over the years. The fact of the matter is that as the world has changed, this board game has been kept up to date as well. This has gone a long way in making Life an enjoyable game for everybody who plays it...
>
> As the years go by, the rules that govern Life are going to change. But instead of worrying about the future, play the version of the game that you have with the rules that are outlined for you. Each game comes with a rule booklet that will help you to get started if you are struggling."

Did you notice the implications for today's leader in those paragraphs? Consider. . .

- Life has changed a lot over the years
- "Old school" is out, core skills (people skills) are in (the world has changed)

- Your growth as a leader is critical to your success (keeping up to date)
- When you are growing it makes work more enjoyable for *everyone* around you
- Life is changing so fast that worrying about the future will take you out of enjoying today
- When you are struggling, tap into your support system (to help you get started)

According to Merriam-Webster, the word "game" comes from the Old High German meaning for *amusement*. By definition then, a game is *"any activity undertaken or regarded as a contest involving rivalry, strategy, or struggle."*

"Any activity" could be your business. It could even be your leadership approach.

If being a leader is viewed as a game, then your company, your business, and your department will be impacted.

Let's do a quick exercise. On a scale of 1 to 6 (1= Never; 6=Most of the time), *how would you rank your experience as a leader* in terms of the following statements?

1. Work is *a contest;* the mentality has become "us vs. them" *within* or with your team.
2. You wear your *game face;* who you really are is being lost in the intensity.
3. The *game plan* is pushing back against your values, ethics, truth, character, relationships.
4. The players (people) are pawns you use in your effort to win.
5. *Mind games* are employed to manipulate, intimidate or confuse others.

6. The *focus of the game* is on who loses; so self-preservation takes over.
7. The *name of the game* has subtly shifted from purpose, passion, and mission.
8. The *scoreboard* has people "kissing up" to you *or* you're kissing up.
9. Work is a *shell game;* what has little value is replacing what you once valued highly.

What do you see or hear in your answers? What concerns you the most?

What happens when you accept your leadership opportunity as a gift?

According to Merriam-Webster, the word "gift" comes from the Old English meaning *to give.* A gift is *"something voluntarily transferred by one person to another without compensation."*

What does it take to embrace leadership as a gift that is to be received and nurtured?

Consider these three responses, which when cultivated, can help you keep in today's world as a leader that people want to follow:

1. **Humility** – unchecked pride suggests a successful leader is "self-made." Really? Of course you have personal responsibility and commitments to develop yourself, but humility allows you to acknowledge the investment of others in your life, as well.

2. **Appreciation** – the very nature of "leadership as a game" can lead to devaluing others. Showing appreciation for the support and contribution of others with your words and actions is powerful and important. Remember your ability to lead is a *cultivated gift.* Appreciation is about

assigning true value to your greatest asset—people in your world.

3. **Gratitude** – beyond appreciation is expressing thanks for what others do to contribute to the success of your company, organization, department, project . . . *your* success.

What happens when you see your leadership as a **gift**?

- You see the people and lead accordingly
- Your followership is increased
- Your influence is extended
- Performance is improved

Your Personal Reflection

- ❖ What best describes your worldview on leadership: is it a gift or a game?

- ❖ Who has had a significant impact on your leadership development? Do they know?

- ❖ The pace of life seeks to hinder the expression of gratitude. How will you "thank" the people who make things happen day in and day out?

๑12๑

Insanity is Optional

The German-born American physicist, Albert Einstein, is given credit for the words often used to paint a picture of insanity: *"doing the same thing over and over again and expecting different results."*

Insanity is another way of saying poor performance, or that someone is "stuck."

Albert's simple definition clearly exposes how individuals can consistently underperform in work or life. To "expect" a different outcome or to hope for improved performance does not make it so. Improved performance, *the end of doing "less well than expected,"* is possible when you change ineffective, unproductive behavior.

Mark was the vice president of marketing and sales for a privately held company. Over the course of our coaching engagement, we began to identify what was getting in his way. For example, each time he started a new initiative, he was often overly optimistic about what he and his team could accomplish, as well as the potential upside for the company. Once the decision was made to move forward, execution became a problem leading to missed goals.

He was so *busy* he took on projects without considering existing priorities. Often he covered for someone on his team, "a nice guy" but accountability was minimized. Lack of focus dominated team planning meetings. Over the course of several months, we were able to identify replacement behaviors.

Here are a few of the changes he began using to improve his performance:

- **Reflection:** Creating a time and a place that allowed him to slow down, gain clarity, and make better decisions.
- **Core Motive:** He discovered what drove his behavior; this allowed him to leverage this driving force instead of pushed around by it.
- **Expectation Setting:** He adopted a four-step process (Communication, Commitment, Consequences, and Coaching) and enjoyed greater clarity with his boss, his peers, and his subordinates.
- **Delegation:** He changed his thinking about the role of delegation. No longer "dumping on others," he began to see "developmental opportunities" for emerging leaders.
- **Asking Questions:** This foundation to great leadership improves performance. He adopted the mantra "Ask more, Tell Less, Teach When You Can." Learning to frame open-ended questions is a key skill for every leader.

If you're experiencing leadership insanity, consider the following:

1. Where is current performance unacceptable, where are you stuck?
2. Schedule time for consistent reflection and notice what is going on around you.
3. How is your behavior impacting others, the situation; what's getting in your way?
4. What change would make a difference? What might you stop doing? Start doing?
5. Rally your support system to get it done.

After my coaching engagement with Mark came to an official end, I called the owner of the company to follow up on Mark's progress.

The owner confirmed significant improvement in Mark's leadership.

It was Mark's willingness to reflect on reality that allowed him to **stop the insanity** and **accelerate** his leadership development.

Remember: Insanity is optional; but so is improved performance.

Your Personal Reflection

- ❖ As a leader, what are you doing that may be holding you back from your full potential?

- ❖ When do you practice consistent reflection?

- ❖ Where do you see insanity in your leadership? Your organization's leaders?

❧13❧

The Productivity Battle

Not long ago, I was privileged enough to sit with Jim Stovall. If you don't know Jim, he has overcome blindness to become one of the world's most successful motivational and leadership experts, entrepreneurs, and authors. He is Co-Founder and President of the Emmy Award-winning Narrative Television Network, and the author of several books, including the 4-million bestseller, *The Ultimate Gift*, which was made into a feature-length movie starring James Garner.

One of his many gifts that morning was a copy of *Ultimate Productivity: A Customized Guide to Discovering your Personal Path to Success.* Steve Forbes wrote in the Foreword:

> "... Jim strikes at the heart of success and failure for all of us individually and as a society. Natural and human resources abound, but how we harness them to create our own personal success is determined by our ingenuity and productivity."

Productivity must deal with illusion, deception, and reality.

What exactly does the productivity battle involve?

- **The Illusion:** "You will have **time** for that later."
- **The Deception:** "Wow, you sure are **busy**!"
- **The Reality:** "You will succeed because you are **engaged** in what **matters** most *right now*."

The Illusion deals with time.

When you accept a misleading view of time, you make poor choices, waste time, and increase your stress. The message "**Later**...*that can wait*" is designed to encourage procrastination. When "later" comes it is then that you realize the time wasted. *The Illusion* returns to mock you for falling for the same old trick yet again.

This moment in time will **never** repeat—that is the truth. This hour, your morning, this day of life will never happen again. Productivity calls us to be good stewards of time; used wisely, intentionally, purposefully, and energize it by your passion and you have an impact.

The Deception is about busy.

Deception imposes a false understanding regarding your time use leading to a lack of awareness, misunderstanding, and even vulnerability. If you accept the message that "being busy" is what matters, your efforts will be to stay busy. Busy gets in the way of adding value. Yes, busy feels good. Reflection seems wasteful. That is part of the deceptive plan.

When your days are full of activity, you **lose freedom to receive something greater**. Being busy about the "wrong things" will land you where you don't want to be. As Jim Stovall writes, *"Just because you are moving does not mean you are moving in the right direction."*

Reality: You will succeed as you do what matters the most, at this moment.

Reality is doing the right thing, for the right reason, at the right time, for the good of all. Reality is about what is real, *not* illusionary or deceptive.

Productivity is about being engaged in what really matters. Being productive is about producing results. Success comes because you are engaged in **what matters most *now*.**

The Secret to Productivity is to *recognize* **the illusion of time** and **the deception of too busy** in order to live in **the reality of what matters most, right now.** Such a response will lead to future success.

To summarize, **the illusion** is "I'll have time *later*."

The deception is about being "*busy*."

The **reality** is: you will succeed because *right now*, you are engaged in what matters most.

> "*In a ready, aim, fire world, too often we overlook the ready and aim portions of the equation. There's only one good reason to pursue any activity, and that is because it's the most productive and efficient way to accomplish your mission of moving toward your personal success goal.*"
>
> *– Jim Stovall, Ultimate Productivity*

In Stovall's book, he tells of an opportunity to train a team of salespeople. The people worked on commission with no other responsibilities other than to sell their products. As he observed them, they appeared to be working very hard: arriving early, a lot of activity, and often staying late. Then he asked them some questions. Here are four edited questions he asked:

1. How many hours a week do you work?
2. How hard are you working?
3. What is your job here?

4. How could you accomplish your job, other than by the way you are currently working at it?

The only way they succeeded was to connect with prospects. Their assignment was to track, using a stopwatch, the actual time they engaged a prospect (their productivity measure). Once they reached 15 hours of productivity, they were done until the next week.

Some months later, feedback came in:

- A third were breaking sales records
- A third were still working forty-five hours a week
- A third had quit; they could not handle the unstructured freedom and responsibility

Remember...

The **Illusion** voice says, "You'll have time for that, later," while the **Deception** message is, "You are so very busy, good job!" **Reality** clarifies the *truth* by saying, "**You will succeed, because right now you are engaged in what will produce results.**"

Your Personal Reflection

❖ What do you desire to accomplish with your life? What are your thoughts about "time"... your lifetime?

❖ Where do you think you are "wasting time"? What causes you to procrastinate?

❖ What is it costing you to live "busy"? How will you engage in "what matters most" *today?*

☙14☙

The Fleeting Nature of Life

I was on my way to see Wendell. Riding the elevator to the 7th floor, I wasn't sure what to expect. His wife Bonnie, his son Kent, and other family members were there, too. Wendell was one of those great individuals who loved life, loved people, and *everyone* else loved—for over 92 years.

His battle with cancer intensified, and it was now apparent that he was living his last weeks at St. Francis Hospital. Every doctor and nurse loved Wendell, you could just tell. In March, he was going to be 93 years old. But he would not make it . . . he was *"going Home."*

When I was leaving the hospital, a nurse entered the main entrance, with her patient's mandatory wheelchair ride to the car completed. As I watched the young woman get into the back seat, I knew her life would be different. Her husband smiled and waved as he pulled away from the curb, a happy chauffeur to his wife and their newborn baby—they were *going Home.*

Life ends and begins.

How to maximize these brief years of life takes me back to my conversation with Jim Stovall. His book, *Ultimate Productivity: A Customized Guide to Discovering your Personal Path to Success,* fuels my commitment to pursue and enjoy greater productivity; it stimulates my thinking and sense of responsibility.

With today's information overload, technology-based connectivity, expectations to do more with less, and basic time poverty comes an environment of distractions.

To be productive, it is critical to distinguish the internal messages; each voice seeks to guide your **decision making** process regarding how you spend your life.

As discussed . . .

The Voice of Illusion says, "You'll have time for that, *later.*"
The Voice of Deception repeats, "You are very busy, *good job!*"
The Voice of Reality clarifies *truth*: "You will succeed when you choose, right now, to engage in what will *produce results.*"

What is required to maintain your focus on doing what matters most?

1. Respect Life's Fleeting Nature

The pace of life seeks to control your life; when successful, it accelerates the fleeting nature of time. When was the last time you considered your life's story line—where you started, where you are, and where you want to be? Mid-course corrections are essential.

Being mindful of how limited time is can serve you well and lead to increased productivity. It is the classic "week before vacation" story. What drives high productivity in that week prior to an extended out-of-office time? The voice of truth pushes you to get the important stuff done *now.*

> *"Time is the quality of nature that keeps events from happening all at once. Lately it doesn't seem to be working."*
> *– Anonymous*

2. Re-frame Work as Creative Opportunity

Productivity is about having the power to produce, delivering results, benefits, or profits; it is being effective in bringing something into existence. Your contribution adds value.

What happens when you view your work as creative activity? Being productive speaks to the artist in you. Your performance makes something that would not be otherwise.

> *"Creativity comes from trust. Trust your instincts. And never hope more than you work."*
> – Rita Mae Brown

3. Recognize the Power of Making Progress

What happens on a great workday? What makes you enthusiastic about your work? The list can include the common responses of recognition, incentives, purpose, passion, being valued, clear goals. How about progress?

Independent researchers, Teresa Amabile and Steven Kramer, completed a multi-year study tracking the day-to-day activities, emotions, and motivational levels of workers. Their article, "What Really Motivates Workers," from the *Harvard Business Review*, suggests the following answer (emphasis added):

> "It's *progress*. On days when workers have the sense they're making headway in their jobs, or when they receive support that helps them overcome obstacles, their emotions are most positive and their **drive to succeed is at its peak**. On days when they feel they are *spinning their wheels or encountering roadblocks to meaningful accomplishment*, their moods and motivation are lowest."

> "...**making progress** in one's work – even incremental progress – is more frequently associated with **positive emotions** and **high motivation** than any other workday event."

When you remove barriers that hinder a sense of *making progress*, your reward is increased motivation and productivity.

4. Retaining Personal Responsibility for Results

When your "why" is big, the desired outcome fuels a sense of responsibility which supports your decision to do what matters most, *right now*. The narrow focus on results can lead to the "end justifies the means" mentality—get it done, no matter what.

Connecting a **moment of decision** to your future success supports this commitment to do what matters most. Accepting authority to make such decisions is critical to productivity. When you attach personal responsibility for results to your vision, mission, and purpose, your decisions will lead to personal success.

Your personal success increases when you decide to do what matters most, right now. You can make those decisions by:

- Respecting the fleeting nature of life
- Reframing your work as a creative opportunity
- Recognizing how motivation comes as you make progress
- Retaining personal accountability for results

Wendell's journey ended just shy of 93 years on earth. At the same time, the path toward success began for a newborn person.

Your personal success and mission fulfillment are at stake; choose wisely.

Your Personal Reflection

❖ How do you rate yourself on the following four supports of productivity?

1 = "Huh?"; 2 ="That makes sense"; 3 ="That makes sense"; 4 = "I'm so there!"

_____ Respecting life's fleeting nature
_____ Reframing work as creative opportunity
_____ Recognizing the power of making progress
_____ Retaining personal responsibility for results

❖ What would you accomplish today if you were leaving for vacation tomorrow?

❖ How can you associate that "procrastinated task" to your personal success? What is hindering your progress today?

❧15❧

Choosing Reality

It was an informal re-connecting conversation with Brian, as his coaching engagement with me concluded several months prior. However, staying in touch with clients is an important and rewarding aspect of my work as a coach.

That day we discussed personal productivity and personal success.

As discussed, three voices seek to influence your thoughts and, thus, **decision-making** in an attempt to take hostage your future success. They do so by seeking to influence your use of time.

Your personal success increases as you determine to do what matters most, *right now.* The suggestion is that it is easier to make wise decisions when you live today:

- Respecting the fleeting nature of life
- Reframing work as creative opportunity
- Receiving motivation from making progress
- Retaining personal accountability for results

During my discussion with Brian that day, he raised a great question: *What can I do, what techniques will help me become more productive?*

Here are three ideas.

1. Schedule an Interruption

As a young kid, I would walk to the playground. Whether it was for 1on1 hoops or flag football, it was easy for me to lose track of time. Perhaps you can think back of an activity from your childhood that caused you to lose yourself in time.

What happens when you start "researching" using Google? How often does that 10-minute task expand and you wonder where did the hour go?

Just think of all those hyperlinks. No wonder it is so easy to spend a lot of time in web-based research. Right? The "deceptive voice" cheers you on, reinforcing your behavior with, *"You're so busy, good job!"* It feels so good, so productive. But remember: activity is only productive when you are active doing what matters most.

This is where a "scheduled interruption" can come in handy. Set your smart phone timer or an egg timer for a reasonable amount of time for the project. The timer simply tells you to check-in and ask: *Are you still doing what matters most, right now?* You create a little space so you can make a decision about what to do next.

2. Use a 4-D Inquiry

No, this is not a formal investigation regarding your personal productivity.

What happens when you develop the habit of asking questions? Communication is improved. What happens when you develop the habit of asking yourself questions? Communication is further improved, which can increase your productivity.

For example, what might happen if you ask yourself the following throughout your day?

- How does what I am doing *right now* help me achieve personal success?
- What am I to do with this (report, piece of mail, e-mail, request, etc.)?
- If I make this new commitment, what will I need to stop doing?

The personal Q-n-A regarding time will lead to increased productivity.

3. Live in Real Time

Real time is the actual time during which something happens. In productivity, this is about being aware of what is going on with your time, schedule, and focus in the moment.

This concept is the basis of the Emmy and Golden Globe award winning show, *24*, starring Kiefer Sutherland. As you may know, the story unfolds over the course of one day—a very full day! The script and commercial breaks happen as if in real time. With every episode you are keenly aware of what time it is—and that time is running out.

To live in the moment, to be present, to focus is to live in real time. Knowing **why** you are doing **what** you are doing is critical to staying on course and increased productivity. Clarity here strengthens your resolve to do what matters most, right now in real time.

On the day I met with Brian, he reported that the 4-D Inquiry was helping him improve his productivity.

Remember: productivity is the result of choosing reality over an illusion regarding the use of time.

Your Personal Reflection

❖ When do you spend more time than you originally planned? What is the activity?

❖ How will you develop the habit of a personal Q-n-A session around your day?

❖ How will you incorporate the 4-D Inquiry?

❧16❧

The Fastball

Few people have the ability to throw a small round object over 60 feet within a defined 17-inch wide space somewhere between an individual's knees and chest. The ability to place a pitch precisely in the strike zone earns professional baseball pitchers sizable contracts.

The tricky part of the "strike zone" is that it changes with each batter. There is no automatic strike zone and much of what is a strike or not a strike is the judgment of the home plate umpire. Impressive when you consider a fastball travels at a speed of 95 to 100 mph.

When it comes to the fastest pitcher, the most widely held response remains Nolan Ryan. His fastball, officially clocked by the *Guinness Book of World Records*, reached 100.9 miles per hour when the California Angels were defeated by the Detroit Tigers, on August 20, 1974, in Anaheim Stadium.

Controlling the Need to Control

While a pitcher must control his pitch, an effective leader understands the negative effect of an *unchecked* need to control. Your ability to *release* control supports performance.

While management does involve exercising power or authority over something, an **excessive** need to control is unproductive and creates performance issues.

Have you ever noticed the challenge a new manager faces? I call this the *next level* transition—moving from a narrow *personal* success focus to *achieving success with and through others.* It is *next level* leadership that moves from technical, practical understanding *to* increased influence. This is the reason a successful sales professional may fail as a sales manager.

An excessive need to control your department or company will lead to living out of control. Control is an illusion. Excessive control lowers performance, yours and that of the people you need to be successful.

> *"No man will make a great leader who wants to do it all himself, or to get all the credit for doing it."*
> *– Andrew Carnegie*

What does it mean to "control"?

Consider the following shades of meaning the *Encarta Thesaurus* offers for control:

- manage (v.) – organize, be in charge of, run, have power over, be in command of, direct
- power (n.) – jurisdiction, rule, domination
- rule (v.) – manipulate, influence, dominate, oppress, have a hold over, hold sway over, dictate
- restrain (v.) – keep under control, keep in check, hold back, rein in, contain
- monitor (v.) – check, regulate, inspect, limit restrict
- influence (n.) – command, say, sway

Although this list is incomplete, the message is clear, excessive control hinders productivity. Consider how it:

- Stifles creativity

- Lowers morale
- Increases stress for *everyone*
- Interferes with *open* communication
- Hinders superior performance
- Reduces the possibility of trust
- Increases the frustration of everyone
- Leads to turnover of motivated and talented people
- Deteriorates your credibility
- Diminishes your influence
- Interferes with teamwork & collaboration
- Limits the helpful aspect of "managing up"
- Weakens relationships
- Keeps others from developing and growing their skills

Clearly set expectations are critical to performance.

To release control is an **act of liberation** from a self-imposed burden—trying to control situations, the process, the project, or the people. Once free, the power to accomplish more is immediate as you tap into the ability and strength of others. Is there anything on this list you don't desire for your operation?

1. Increased creativity
2. Improved morale
3. Reduced stress
4. Open communication lines
5. Improved performance
6. Enlarged trust
7. Increasing job-related satisfaction
8. Retaining motivated and talented people
9. Enhanced credibility with your team
10. Your circle of influence grows
11. Greater team work and collaboration
12. Acceptance of feedback and supportive "managing up"
13. Stronger relationships
14. Consistent personal growth and skill development

Once this restriction on your future success is eliminated—the need to control—others will contribute and succeed, too. By releasing control, everybody wins.

Your Personal Reflection

- ❖ Take a moment to review the section on **"What does it mean to "control?"** Which of the descriptors or behaviors best describes what you want?

- ❖ How does the "desire to control" show up in **your behavior**?

- ❖ Which of the **positive outcomes** associated with releasing control would improve the performance of your team, department, or company?

❧17❧

The Irony of Excessive Control

The most recent meeting Sara had with her manager became an instructive story. During our coaching conversation, she reflected on the experience and the application became clear to her. She understood her *core motive*—**to be in control**.

Sara realized how her core motive drove her thinking, behavior, and ultimately her performance. Now aware of this need to control, she was able to choose to be intentional and pro-active.

Sara is now learning how to take a deep breath, evaluate what she is thinking, and *release control*. Her performance is improving, and she has the freedom to use her strengths as she gets out of her own way. Everyone is capable of this.

However, when *unaware* of her core motive, Sara is reactionary and unintentional in her behavior. All of us are. Her need to control pushes the *out-of-control* use of her strengths, resulting in unproductive behavior and people conflict.

Sara's story centered on a feedback conversation. Her control-oriented manager was frustrated and telling Sara, with emotional intensity, all about what she was doing wrong. The manager was out of control.

However, if I were to have asked the manager, she probably would have denied it. She may have been the only person in the room who didn't understand her behavior—a *behavioral hostage*.

Eventually, Sara told me of the statement her boss made to her, *"It's a good thing I didn't come to your office yesterday or I would have walked you out the door right then."*

Why control the impulse to "control"?

Keith Ayers, in *Engagement is Not Enough*, writes about how managers can unintentionally increase the disengagement of their employees. His short list includes:

1. An obsession with financial results
2. An obsession with control
3. An obsession with avoiding responsibility
4. An obsession with logic

He correctly observes the lack of research to support a control-based approach to leadership and management. How does a control-oriented leader show up? Ayers points, summarized here, are insightful. Such leaders (emphasis added):

- Assume that **people cannot be trusted** and send that message to their team
- **Micromanage** employees, believing that tasks will not be completed to their standards unless they are checking in on their teams
- Assume employees **do not really want to work**, and therefore they need to continue to drive them to achieve results
- Believe that, as the manger, they have all the knowledge and experience, and therefore they need to make all the decisions about how to improve performance

Notice how leaders who seek excessive control display out-of-control behavior, all the while living with the illusion of being in control. What does that look like?

Consider the emotional statement Sara's boss made to her about firing her on the spot. Yes, it was out of control. To this manager's credit, she did apologize later.

Apology accepted. Nevertheless, how do you think this exchange affected Sara's engagement as an employee? How would it affect yours?

How committed is this emerging leader to an environment where the potential of "one wrong move and you're out of here" is implied? Furthermore, how does this behavior create an obstacle to Sara's ability and willingness to support her manager's success?

Influence vs. Control

Leaders who **release control** demonstrate **self-control** and gain **influence.**

Influence allows support to flow to you instead of trying to force control; it is about collaborating instead of commanding.

- Influence is the *freedom* to have a positive effect on others
- Influence allows you to *capture* the devotion and allegiance of others
- Influence allows you to achieve your goals
- Influence is the freedom from trying to prove you are in charge, allowing everyone to contribute and enjoy success

Great performance comes from an environment where great people have an opportunity to contribute their unique perspective, talent, and voice to the process, project, or job. You cannot control the process, but you can direct it as you communicate the vision, set clear expectations, and define desired outcomes.

To release control is an **act of liberation** from a self-imposed burden. Once free, the power to accomplish more is immediate as you tap into the creativity of others and allow collaboration. Trust, improved morale, open communication, employee engagement, and improved performance are your reward.

How does it happen?

It requires a change in *leadership behavior.*

The irony is that leaders who **release control** demonstrate **self-control** and **gain influence.**

> *"Be not angry that you cannot make others as you wish them to be, since you cannot make yourself as you wish to be."*
>
> *– Thomas Kempis*

Your Personal Reflection

- ❖ What kind of work environment are you creating for your team to operate in every day?

- ❖ What are the benefits of releasing control?

- ❖ What has been your experience with control-oriented leaders?

☙18❧

The Prudent Leader

When was the last time you heard the word "prudent" in a leadership development conversation? Perhaps you will be surprised at just how appropriate it is.

Consider these four qualities of a prudent person:

1. **Resource Management**: smart use of assets.
2. **Common Sense**: ability to deal with practical matters.
3. **Foresight**: sound judgment that helps you consider likely consequences and make adjustments to minimize risk.
4. **Self-discipline**: powerful ability to govern and discipline oneself using reason.

Prudence is about the ability to handle practical matters with good judgment. Whether you are leading your life, a department, or an entire company, prudence is a necessary leadership skill.

How do we become prudent?

This ancient proverb lends the secret . . .

> *"The wisdom of the prudent is to give thought to their ways; the folly of fools is deception."*

This proverb brings emphasis to a reflective personal growth path. This leads to my own personal philosophy:

The best predictor of continued success is the ability and willingness to learn and change achieved through consistent reflection on truth found in the story.

Reflection, thinking, and writing, supports the success of my executive coaching process. It's a key discipline of successful people. If you desire **accelerated** personal development, you can increase this practice by creating space.

Wisdom teaches us to give thought to our ways. The reward is insight that leads to changed behavior, improved performance, and observable results—growth!

Another word associated with prudence is "foresight," which brings together the ideas of wisdom, insight, and knowledge. Wikipedia notes:

> "In this (foresight) case, the virtue is the ability to judge between virtuous and vicious actions, not only in a general sense, but with regard to appropriate actions at a given time and place."

Leading your life, department, or organization is greatly enhanced when you have the ability to choose wisely. The big payoff of consistent reflection is a growing ability to execute.

What if prudence is minimized?

Returning to the Hebrew proverb, we find what happens if we fail to cultivate this virtue. While the wisdom of the prudent is to give thought to their ways, "the folly of fools is *deception*."

Deception is the practice of leading someone to believe something that is not true. When someone deliberately hides the truth from us, our freedom is hindered.

Deception impacts our thinking, then our beliefs, expectations, attitude, behavior, and ultimately our performance. Success flows out of freedom and freedom comes from knowing the truth.

Of course, we can work to convince ourselves of something that is not true, as well as self-deceive. But the result is the same—loss of freedom and limited success.

Being prudent is about creating space in our "busy lives" so that we may give thought to our lives to support our personal growth and development in order to have high impact.

When you engage your head and heart in careful thought about your story, you will discover truth; truth will liberate you from limiting behaviors bringing growth; growth leads to improved performance and results—success happens.

Your Personal Reflection

❖ How do you rate yourself on these four qualities of a prudent leader?

1. The smart use of assets.
2. The ability to deal with practical matters.
3. The use of sound judgment in order to consider likely consequences and make adjustments to minimize risk.
4. The powerful ability to govern and discipline oneself using reason.

❖ How well are you giving thought to your ways?

❖ In which ways can you become a more prudent leader?

Harmony

The New Work-Life Balance

❧19❧

Shark!

Perhaps you saw "Jaws." I didn't, but here's the story line.

Martin Brody is the police chief of Amity, an island resort town somewhere in New England. One summer morning, Brody is called to the beach, where the mangled body of a summer vacationer has washed ashore. The medical examiner tells the chief it could have been a shark that killed the swimmer.

The Mayor, who is desperate to keep the revenue from July 4th tourists wants Brody to say the young woman's death was caused by a motorboat propeller instead of a shark...because the thought of a shark would drive tourists away from Amity.

Shark expert Matt Hooper believes the female swimmer was killed by a shark. Hooper is proven right a few days later, when another person is killed.

Quint, the shark hunter, offers to find the shark and kill it, but Police Chief Vaughn thinks his $10,000 professional service fee is too high. Meanwhile, Mayor Vaughn leaves the beaches open; he still wants the summer revenue.

After another crazy experience, the mayor agrees to hire Quint to find the shark.

Now, take a look at how Quint responds to the mayor's challenge:

Quint: Y'all know me. Know how I earn a livin'. I'll catch this bird for you, but it ain't gonna be easy. Bad fish. Not like going down the pond chasin' bluegills and tommycods. This shark, swallow you whole. Little shakin', little tenderizin', an' down you go.

And we gotta do it quick, that'll bring back your tourists, put all your businesses on a payin' basis. But it's not gonna be pleasant. I value my neck a lot more than three thousand bucks, chief. I'll find him for three, but I'll catch him, and kill him, for ten.

But you've gotta make up your minds. If you want to stay alive, then ante up. If you want to play it cheap and be on welfare for the whole winter.

I don't want no volunteers, I don't want no mates, there's just too many captains on this island. Ten thousand dollars for me by myself. For that you get the head, the tail, the whole damn thing.

When do you yell "Shark!"?

As a certified executive coach and people developer, it is my heartfelt duty to proclaim this warning: **"Business Eats People!"**

Business (your work) will take whatever you are willing to give it and still want more. It's the nature of business to consume and produce . . . consume and produce . . . consume and produce. This is how business functions. It's not good or bad, right or wrong—it's just how it works.

Knowing this to be true, I hope you work at a business that values people (you).

As mentioned earlier, I believe ***the business of business is people***. When a business takes care of its people, the people will take care of the business.

When this is not the case, your work will *"...swallow you whole. Little shakin', little tenderizin', an' down you go."*

Did you just scream "Shark!"?

"Okay, Steve, but what about OSHA?"

Well, let's take a look. OSHA, of course, is the Occupational Safety and Health Administration of the United States. According to Wikipedia, OSHA:

> "...was created by Congress under the Occupational Safety and Health Act signed by President Richard M. Nixon, on December 29, 1970. Its mission is to prevent work-related injuries, illnesses, and occupational fatality by issuing and enforcing standards for workplace safety and health."

As well intentioned and valuable as the mission of this agency may be, OSHA is *not* there to protect your work-life balance. It will *not* encourage you to live out your values or make sure you are engaged in meaningful work or that you are doing work that you enjoy or that allows you to use your strengths.

No one can do this except **you**.

The setting of boundaries, the negotiation of expectations, and making choices that lead to living life with purpose and passion while serving others is our personal responsibility. "The company" or "the boss" will not do it—not even when a business leader says "our most important asset is our people."

Remember: the nature of business is to eat people. It's not right or wrong, it's just how works. Whatever you are willing to sacrifice, it will take.

This is not an attack on "big business" or business "in general" or "capitalism." No profit, no business, no provision. It *is* about being aware of the sign on the beach.

It is about embracing personal responsibility for your personal development, which includes living well.

Perhaps you've experienced the effects of downsizing recently.

The pressure to do more with less is like never before! And with more pressure and greater demands, your work will *"...swallow you whole. Little shakin', little tenderizin', an' down you go."*

There's a man-eating creature out there. How are you **protecting** your personal well-being?

Your Personal Reflection

❖ **Pay attention to your story.** What's the message around hours worked, stress, your health, strain on your relationships? How well are you living out your values?

❖ **Be intentional.** Where can you make an adjustment? What's one thing you can do to "take back your life"?

❖ **Solicit support.** Everyone needs an objective person to ask real questions and encourage the hard choices. Who will you call on for support?

❧20❧

24/7 . . . Really?

I was reconnecting with a former employee. She ran a few minutes late for our 7:05 a.m. breakfast appointment. It was fine, as I enjoyed the wait outside the restaurant on that 68-degree, late summer morning.

Upon arrival, she apologized and explained why she didn't call—her phone was MIA. It wasn't really lost, just not coming out of hiding. Apparently, the battery was drained, so forget the prompt suggestion of "Just call your phone."

Of course, it wasn't really a phone; it was a "Smart Phone"—an intelligent device . . . fashionable. (Yes, I have one.)

My journey to hyper-connectedness started with my Blackberry (model 6230 is an "antique" by today's advanced technology standards; good grief, its all of 6-7 years old).

Yes, I'd heard the stories of people sleeping with their Blackberry and heard the "CrackBerry" jokes. My boss, at the time was thrilled that our management team was going to be connected and responsive.

I can remember when we would let the old "land line" ring when a call came in during dinner and think, "They'll call back." Once upon a time it was considered rude to sit at the table with the privacy curtain of a newspaper cutting you off from others.

Exchange of Information

Communication is about the exchange of information between people; it's delivering a message whether spoken or written or through behavior. I love helping people become better communicators—**people connecting with people**.

There is another meaning to communication that has to do with "access." This is the opportunity to approach or connect to get information. No breaking news here, information is available 24/7, which is giving some traditional delivery systems the challenge of their lifetime.

When is 24/7 access too much?

Tim Ferris provides some interesting stats on his blog, Experiments in Lifestyle Design, around e-mail addiction and information overload. Consider this:

- 66% of people read email seven days a week and expect to receive a response the same day
- 61% continue to check email while on vacation
- 56% have anxiety if they can't access email

"CrackBerry" was the official winner of the 2006 Word-of-the-Year as selected by the editorial staff of Webster's New World College Dictionary. Blackberry addiction has been labeled "similar to drugs" in a study performed by Rutgers University; millions of users are now unable to go more than five minutes without checking e-mail.

According to online surveys of more than 4,000 people, conducted jointly by AOL and the Opinion Research Corporation, and reported in 2005:

- 41% of Americans check e-mail first thing in the morning
- 18% check e-mail right after dinner
- 14% check e-mail right when they get home from work
- 14% check e-mail right before they go to bed
- 40% have checked their e-mail in the middle of the night

More than one in four (26%) say they can't go more than two to three days without checking email, and they check it everywhere:

- In bed - 23%
- In class - 12%
- In business meetings - 8%
- At the beach or pool - 6%
- In the bathroom - 4%
- While driving - 4%
- In church - 1%

Who's been sleepin' in my bed?

The Pew Research Center is a nonpartisan "fact tank" that provides information on the issues, attitudes, and trends shaping America and the world by conducting public opinion polling and social science research.

Their recent report on Millennials provides interesting information on cell phone usage. *The line between work life and personal life is being blurred with each generation, with each new device.* Millennials are being called the first "always-connected" generation in history. According to the report (emphasis added):

> "Millennials are more likely than older Americans to treat their cell phones as a necessary and **important appendage**. Many even bring their cell phones to bed. A majority (57%) of the public has placed their cell phone on or right next to their bed while sleeping." (Page 39)

What's the price of "always connected"?

In 1992, the United Nations declared stress the "20th Century epidemic."

In our fast-paced society, where information overload is commonplace and each day involves hundreds of decisions and interruptions, stress finds a fertile field. Perhaps nowhere is the rise in stress more real than your workplace.

An article on Bank of America's Small Business website suggests,

> "Stress-induced health issues, absenteeism, employee turnover, and lower productivity cost our economy an estimated $300 million a year. On average, according to data from the Center for Economic and Policy Research, adults in the United States work longer hours and take less vacation than workers in any other industrialized nation. Perhaps then, it's no surprise that a recent study of 2,500 American workers by CareerBuilder.com found that more than three out of four-77 percent-feel overworked and burned-out at their jobs."

What are we afraid of?

One of my coaching exercises delivers this powerful truth: **emotion-based fear drives ancient, unproductive behavior, which hinders performance.**

Upon leaving breakfast, my friend suggested she may not replace her "Smart Phone," opting out for "just a cell phone." Why? She was enjoying the freedom.

Your Personal Reflection

- ❖ What "fear" drives your need to be connected 24/7?

- ❖ How do you manage the expectation to be technologically connected 24/7?

- ❖ What is the cost in your life of being "always connected"?

⁊21⁊

Following the Lead of Dr Pepper

A recent blog post led me to re-connect with an "old friend"; yes, of course by e-mail, at first, but in the fight for a more personal connection, we agreed to schedule an ancient experience—**voice to voice**. Here is part of what my friend Allison wrote:

> Hi Steve,
>
> Today was my daughter's first day of kindergarten. My alarm (on my iPhone) went off at 6 A.M. I was tired and didn't want to get up, hit the snooze and checked my email. I then proceeded to scan approximately a dozen emails that came in my inbox since 10:00 P.M. last night when I checked it last. I then began reading your article on over-connectedness and started laughing to myself at the irony of reading this while lying in bed!
>
> Now I'm thinking through your question, "What fear drives this need to be connected 24/7?"
>
> Is it my fear of "not being connected"?
>
> Or, to look at it another way, in my mind about one in seven emails will bring a reward of sorts.
>
> Checking your inbox brings you a sense of being connected when you receive a note from a close friend or an email from an old acquaintance you haven't heard from in a long time. It's always fun to open your email and get a good

referral or business lead isn't it? Better yet, it's exciting to get that email that confirms that the business deal you've been working on for several months is a done deal!

Maybe I'm just looking for a "good feeling" or affirmation. Our family just returned from a week's vacation in Jackson Hole, Wyoming. We didn't take computers but Bob and I both brought our iPhones. We kept our "smart phone connecting" to a minimum, I think?

I appreciate Allison's thoughts regarding what can drive this need to be constantly connected: 1) Reward and 2) Affirmation. What are you looking for?

Dr Pepper Email Management Plan

After thinking about the advice I give to my readers, I set out to examine and adjust my own compulsive commitment to "over-connectedness." My first steps:

1. I turned off two of the four email accounts coming to my iPhone.

2. I explored my *"Dr Pepper Email Management Plan."* If you're not familiar with Dr Pepper's marketing strategy, here is an excerpt from the article Roger Grace wrote in the *Metropolitan News-Enterprise*, a Los Angles daily paper, about Dr Pepper:

   "It was in the 1920s that Dr. Walter Eddy at Columbia University studied the body's metabolism. He discovered that a natural drop in energy occurs about 10:30 a.m., 2:30 p.m. and 4:30 p.m. But he also discovered that if the people in his research study had something to eat or drink at 10, 2 and 4, the energy slump could be avoided.

After Dr. Eddy's research findings were released, Dr Pepper challenged its advertising agency to come up with a theme which would suggest that Dr Pepper should be that 10, 2 and 4 drink which would keep the energy level up. The result was one of the most enduring of Dr Pepper's advertising themes: Drink a bite to eat at 10, 2 and 4."

The Dr Pepper Company pushed the notion that ingestion of sugar at 10, 2 and 4 was actually something healthful. And, of course, parents would want their children to engage in healthful practices.

How would this "craving" for email be satisfied with 10/2/4? Correct—not so well. So I thought about adapting it to 8/10/12/2/4/6/8, but, of course, that left out first thing in the morning and last thing at night. Seriously?

I'm still working to define an adequate schedule for checking email. I even added a step three: I turned off the "you've got mail" alert on my iPhone.

Yes, I recognize these steps are only the beginning. But in doing so, I have created a crevice of space that I didn't have before.

How much space do you have in your life?

As an executive coach, I work with people with a lot on their plate. Intensity shows up. Little or no margin in the schedule; not much time left for personal development.

We talk about "Creating Space." By that, I mean "the disciplined use of time, place, and resources to reflect on the story for truth."

Reflection allows you to examine your life, your thinking, and your performance, and to give careful thought to your behavior and performance. Creating space allows you to examine the path you are taking and make adjustments in line with your purpose, passion, and values.

"Measure your life," advises Seneca. "It just does not have room for so much."

What happens if we fail to create space?

This "Creating Space" for consistent reflection is the secret to personal growth.

A failure to create space leaves us stuck in life. Performance suffers and next level success is sacrificed. Your experience of life lived with purpose and passion while making a difference in the world will be limited. Your health, mental, emotional, and spiritual well-being, your relationships will suffer unless you give yourself the gift of consistent reflection.

Allison closed her email by writing:

> I don't think I've really said anything here significant. I'm pondering all of this because I find this phenomenon extremely interesting, as if we're witnessing something that has never happened before in our lifetime.
>
> Does this sound dramatic? Maybe so, but I see it stealing away our relationships to some degree. It's the great paradox. Everyone thinks they are "more connected" with computers and smart phones. Texting and Facebook keep

us all in touch with more people. Could more be less? Less faces, more aloneness.

Now I will stop. I'm beginning to sound like Steve Laswell.

Your Personal Reflection

❖ What do you crave that email and other platforms of connectedness seem to supply?

❖ Imagine losing your "smart phone." How would you respond? Why?

❖ How can you go about creating space in your daily routine?

∾22∾

Life Harmony

The conversation around "work-life balance" is very interesting. According to Wikipedia, "work-life balance" was first used as an expression

> "...in the late 1970s to describe the balance between an individual['s] work and personal life. In the United States, this phrase was first used in 1986.
>
> Over the past twenty-five years, there has been a substantial increase in work which is felt to be due, in part, by information technology and by an intense, competitive work environment. Long-term loyalty and a "sense of corporate community" have been eroded by a performance culture that expects more and more from their employees yet offers little security in return."

Can we say that work–life balance is a proper prioritizing between "work" (career and ambition) on one hand and "life" (pleasure, leisure, family and spiritual development) on the other?

How well does *life compartmentalization* work . . . really?

One of my clients is a decade into a successful career, with C-level responsibilities and a beautiful family. His company sees even greater leadership potential and that's why I'm coaching him.

Mike's technical skills are superior; his development opportunity resides in what I call "**core leadership skills,**" i.e. *people skills.*

One of my coaching exercises helps leaders evaluate their Support System. To navigate life's **transitions and transformation,** we all must have the help and encouragement of others. As Mike completed the reflective exercise, he began to wrestle with this concept of "balance."

As I listened and asked questions, Mike sketched a picture that looked like a cross beam with a support in the center and two pans of equal weight suspended on each end.

This is how most people might view the concept of work-life balance. Think about it; what does it take to obtain "stability" with this instrument? Correct—an *even distribution of weight*—balance.

Nevertheless, I find life more complex than what two pans suspended on a balance beam can represent. A different word came to my mind as I listened to Mike's story. I heard the word **harmony.**

According to www.i.word.com/dictionary, **harmony** is defined as "*the combination of simultaneous musical notes in a chord; pleasing or congruent arrangement of parts.*"

Harmony is also defined by www.i.word.com/dictionary as "*an interweaving of different accounts into a single narrative.*"

Seriously, how do you divide life into just two parts: work life and personal life?

Life Harmony is blending the four parts of what I call **the Story:** self, family, community, and work.

Think about it, The Journey begins when we show up as an **individual**; the new member of a **family**; finding our place in

community, where we learn to make our contribution to society through meaningful **work**. That's the story.

Every day life is the challenge to bring harmony to the story. To interweave all the different parts into a single, pleasing, congruent narrative.

The Story is the Story

One of my favorite coaching principles is around "the Story," summed up as:

> Everyone has a Story.
> Every day we add to our Story.
> Today, you will have influence on someone's Story.

Life Harmony *is the interweaving of different accounts into a single narrative.* Imagine your life lived with such harmony and free flow between the many parts.

We have many roles in life. For example, I'm a man, a son, and a brother; a husband, a dad, and a grandpa; an executive coach, a business owner, a speaker, an equipper, and an author; a friend, a neighbor, a resident of Tulsa, and a follower of Jesus Christ—you get the point.

Imagine interweaving personhood, family life, community, and work into a single narrative—the Story. My intent is to invite a different model about how we "do life," something other than "work-Life balance—**life harmony.**

Your Personal Reflection

❖ How many roles do you have in life?

❖ In what way have you separated your life into parts in an attempt to achieve work-life balance?

❖ What do you think about the concept of blending each part of your life together to achieve **life harmony**?

❧23❧

Let's Make Music

My *informal* LinkedIn survey indicates that the language of "work-life balance" doesn't work for most people.

My concern as an executive coach is about helping leaders achieve greater life-success with less stress. So, I'll leave the corporate responsibility to others, such as Texas Instruments.

Texas Instruments made *Fortune Magazine's* "100 Best Companies to Work For" list in 2009. *Working Mother Magazine* named them one of its "100 Best Companies for Working Mothers" for the 14th consecutive year.

According to their Corporate Report, Texas Instruments' work-life programs encompass flexible working options including flex time, compressed work weeks, part-time options, job sharing and telecommuting, as well as options to reduce stress and ease personal life.

There's nothing new here, but Career Builder conducted a nationwide survey to look at the pressure on today's worker and indicators of work addiction.

More than half of workers (52%) reported they put in more than 40 hours a week. Fourteen percent (14%) work more than 50 hours. Thirty-one percent (31%) bring work home at least once a week; one-in-ten (10%) bring home work at least every other day.

For a quarter of the workers, it's difficult to leave the office behind once they leave for the day:

- 24 percent of workers reported that when they're at home or out socially, they're still thinking about work.
- 19 percent often dream about work.
- 16 percent stated that most of their conversations – at work, home or out socially – always tend to focus on work.

Extended workdays and an unwavering focus on business while at home are taking a toll on family relationships:

- 22 percent of workers reported they don't have time to pursue personal interests because they say they're always working.
- 15 percent reported that they would rather be working than at home.
- 12 percent said the amount of time spent on work is causing friction with their family.
- 9 percent are more concerned about approval from their boss than their family.

Workers reported increased stress levels and health complications tied to pressures at work.

- 51 percent of workers reported their workloads have increased over the last six months.
- 27 percent have not taken a personal or sick day in the last few years.

It sounds like many people are growing tired of living "out of balance"; it's hurting important relationships and the health of our work force.

The *Wall Street Journal* picked up on this tension in their article "New Model for Work-Life Balance on Wall Street?" Nick Leopard, age 30, and Andy Blechman, age 27, formed a company called Accordion Partners, which hires out experienced investment bankers by the hour. Why? (emphasis added):

> **"Flexibility**...appeals to a younger generation that rejects the Wall Street ethos that work means **sacrificing a personal life**. "Right now, we're getting a ton of buzz from people that have been at the banks five years and want a change," Blechman said."

Again, my focus is to support individual personal growth, *not* advise corporate policy. Remember who is responsible for how you live life, define success, and conduct your relationships? That's right—you!

What about "Life Harmony"?

Life Harmony is a new model and way of thinking around "work-life balance."

Life Harmony is about **how you write** your story, how your story fits into **the Story** of yourself, your family, your community and co-workers (work).

Life harmony happens when we interweave our roles, our responsibilities, and our relationships into a single narrative *and enjoy it.*

What guides the making of music?

The relative duration of a musical note is the "value" given it. There are whole notes, half notes, and quarter notes; there are more, even a hundred-twenty-eight note (that's short and fast!)

The actual writing of music is known as **notation**:

> "It is the written expression of music notes and rhythms on paper using symbols. When music is written down, the pitches and rhythm of the music is notated, along with instructions on how to perform the music.
>
> Music is created when the value of the notes is performed; including the sound of a distinct pitch, quality, and duration whether vocal or instrumental. Such an arrangement of notes can lead to a pleasing combination of sounds: *harmony*."

Creating life harmony is also supported by our assigned **values**. So the question to ask is: H*ow much do I value this?*

When something is important, it has great value or worth to us. Whether "work-life balance" or "Life Harmony," knowing and living according to our values helps guide life harmony.

Your Personal Reflection

❖ How well is your life guided by your values? Where do you see conflict?

❖ How is your "work-life balance" affecting important relationships and your health?

❖ How can you tap into your values to create Life Harmony? What's "one thing" you can do today?

~24~

Slow Down to Accelerate

What is the pace of your life these days?

This is a question I often pose in a group coaching session. Here are some of the responses leaders give:

- Speed of light
- Rough
- Busy
- Laid back due to uncertainty/change
- Adapting to circumstances
- Crazy
- Extremely fast, no down time
- Comfortable
- Usually fast, slowing it forcibly
- Fast and Furious

As you review the list, where do you identify?

I appreciate Peter Bregman's candor in his *Harvard Business Review* blog post, "Why I Returned My iPad" (emphasis added):

> "A little more than a week after buying the iPad, I returned it to Apple. The problem wasn't the iPad exactly, though it has some flaws. The problem was me.
>
> I like technology, but I'm not an early adopter. I waited for the second-generation iPod, the second-generation iPhone, and the second-generation MacBook Air.

But the iPad was different. So sleek. So cool. So transformational. And, I figured, since it's so similar to the iPhone, most of the kinks would already be worked out.

So at 4 PM on the day the 3G iPad was released, for the first time in my life, I waited in line for two hours to make a purchase.

I set up my iPad in the store because I wanted to make sure I could start using it the very moment I bought it. And use it I did. I carried it with me everywhere; it's so small and thin and light, why not bring it along?

I did my email on it, of course. But I also wrote articles using Pages. I watched episodes of *Weeds* on Netflix. I checked the news, the weather, and the traffic. And, of course, I proudly showed it to, well, anyone who indicated the least bit of interest.

It didn't take long for me to encounter the dark side of this revolutionary device: it's too good.

It's too easy. Too accessible. Both too fast and too long-lasting. Certainly there are some kinks, but nothing monumental. For the most part, it does everything I could want. Which, as it turns out, is a problem.

Sure I might *want* to watch an episode of Weeds before going to sleep. But should I? It really is hard to stop after just one episode. And two hours later, I'm entertained and tired, but am I really better off? Or would it have been better to get seven hours of sleep instead of five?

The brilliance of the iPad is that it's the anytime-anywhere computer. On the subway. In the hall, waiting for the elevator. In a car on the way to the airport. **Any free moment becomes a potential iPad moment.**

The iPhone can do roughly the same thing, but not exactly. Who wants to watch a movie in bed on an iPhone?

So why is this a problem? It sounds like I was super-productive. **Every extra minute, I was either producing or consuming."**

Sound familiar?

The next question I ask the group is this: *How is this pace affecting your life?* Their answers are telling:

- Impacts my outlook on life
- My health
- Lacking a sense of direction
- Miss-focused, not concentrating on what is important
- Feeling short-changed
- Feeling out of control
- Exhausted
- Questioning: Where am I? Who am I?
- Loss of contentment
- Drinking more Red Bull
- Loss of quality
- Out of balance
- Hurting my performance
- Impacting my life
- Hard on relationships

Life is accelerated, everything seems to happen faster, develop faster, change faster. And the faster our life's pace is, the harder the impact on our lives.

The fundamental purpose of both my personal and group coaching sessions is teaching people how to change their behavior and achieve **personal growth.** Eventually, they learn: **the way to accelerate personal growth is to** *slow life down.*

Your Personal Reflection

❖ What happens when you are overly occupied with activity? What's the impact of being so committed to something that you are unable to undertake another activity of a greater value?

❖ When does your schedule seem ridiculous...to the point that it's not practical or showing good sense, "it's crazy"? What is that costing you?

❖ What's one thing that is so doable it's laughable? What can you do that will help slow life down?

❧25❧

What is the Story Telling You?

Imagine the work required to move a large solid wood dining room table, chairs, and all the other pieces of furniture out of the dining room. Imagine unloading book shelves, a large desk, and a piano out of a study. Imagine the mess created to tear out the wood floor laid only 2-3 years ago.

Imagine the mess and noise created as new wood floor is installed and sanded. Imagine the smell that comes from re-staining and being driven out of your home as the finish coats are applied to the new wood floor.

Now, imagine what you would like to have done with the money spent on re-placing that nearly new, solid oak, wood floor. Okay, the cost may not have funded a vacation to Hawaii; still, the inconvenience of the process just described is not cool—especially if it can be avoided.

Imagine a musty smell as you pass through the laundry room on your way to the garage. Imagine noticing your wood floor starting to cup in a few places and wondering about it. Imagine **you noticed . . . but did nothing.**

Return to paragraph one; that's what it takes to fix it—*now!*

Can you imagine noticing all those indicators but instead of ignoring them you stopped and asked yourself a few simple questions? The answers allowed you to track down the source of the musty smell—a stopped up floor drain in the garage where your air conditioning coil dumps the condensation during humid summer days. (You know what? There is a lot of water extracted from humid air.)

Now, where does a steady stream of water go when it can't leave via the assigned route, the floor drain? It silently seeps between the concrete and ¾-inch plywood. The plywood absorbs the water and shares it with the ¾-inch solid oak wood floor in the dining room and study.

What does water do, given time, to wood flooring? It warps, cups, expands, and RUINS it!

Here's a tip for you: once a tree is no longer a tree it is best to keep water away from it unless you want a very rustic look with your hardwood floor!

What's the point of this true story? Yes, remember to check your condensation pipe and floor drain each spring. Ah, but there is more.

How well are you paying attention to life's feedback? In this story, the **feedback** arrived as a musty smell, moisture in the garage and a little cupping of my wood floor.

Why so much damage? I was busy and didn't take time to reflect on the feedback. I missed the message behind all the feedback until the damage was done.

What do I have now? **Experience!** Along with new wood floors, less cash in my pocket, and the associated hassles.

What have I learned? Check the air conditioner line and floor drain each spring to be sure they are draining properly. Ah, but there is more.

The best predictor of future success is the ability and willingness to learn and change through consistent reflection on truth delivered through the Story.

Feedback comes from various sources; for example, what might be the message from:

- A bounced check or late fees?
- A relationship that is filled with conflict?
- Trouble sleeping at night?
- Not enjoy "going to work" anymore?
- Your habit of finishing other people's sentences for them?
- Your reality: "They can never get it 'right' at the office"?
- High turnover in your division?
- Less laughter and more wrinkles on your forehead?

Your future success is predictable if you have time and a place to consistently reflect on experience, feedback, success, and failure—especially failure. And if you have a support system that encourages your ability and willingness to learn and change, then success is in your future!

Your Personal Reflection

- ❖ So what feedback is life sending you these days? How busy are you? What will the damage be?

- ❖ What if you're so busy you don't hear or see the feedback? What might that cost you?

- ❖ How can you avoid some of life's mess?

≈26≈

The Accelerator of Personal Success

There's no question, most people are living a crazy, fast, 'speed of light' lifestyle.

But there is a price to be paid for this pace. It will show up in the decline of physical, mental, emotional, or spiritual health . . . lack of direction, an out-of-balance work-life, excessive stress, or relationship strain. Everything seems to happen faster, develop faster, change faster.

How do you *accelerate* personal growth?

Growth indicates greater maturity and the associated ability to manage life; and the reward? Greater peace, joy, happiness, fulfillment, engagement, and love along the journey.

The way to accelerate personal growth is to **slow life down.**

Once you take steps to "slow life down," how do you accelerate success?

Here's what my coaching groups say:

- Learn from others
- Pay attention to your inner self
- Gain knowledge
- Seek out and embrace opportunities for experience
- Listen and pay attention to surroundings
- Develop a hunger and dig

- Urgency + Accountability + Time
- Be a sponge
- Learn from those around me

This is not the first time you've read my soon to be famous quote:

> *The Best Predictor of Future Success is the ability and willingness to learn and change achieved through consistent reflection on truth found in the Story.*

Read it again. What do you notice, hear, or feel in that statement?

When you engage your head and heart in careful thought about your Story, you discover truth. Truth liberates from limiting behaviors bringing growth, growth leads to improved performance, and results . . . lead to success!

The Path of Continued Success is summed up in this:

1. To accelerate personal growth, **slow life down**
2. Success in life requires **consistent reflection**

Consistent reflection is the discipline of giving **careful thought** to what's going on in life...the story. **Creating space** for reflective thinking *and* writing allows you to reconsider previous actions, events, decisions, feedback, experience, success, or failure...the story.

What is your reward for this reflection on the story? Truth. By that I simply mean the facts or **reality**. Only when you discover the truth will you live in freedom.

How does the old saying go? *If you tell the truth, you have nothing to fear* . . . you are free.

Fear-based emotions trigger limiting behavior, which undermines continued success. Consistent reflection on the story brings truth and truth gives freedom as you embrace reality, take responsibility, and do the right thing for the right reasons.

Your Personal Reflection

❖ When do you create **time and place** for reflection? How consistent are you?

❖ Where would you like to go in your life? How will you get there?

❖ Where will you create space in your life for consistent reflection?

ॐ27ॐ

Embracing the Teacher We Love to Hate

Yes, I was so looking forward to the presentation. But . . .

The American Society of Training and Development's annual statewide conference was on campus at the University of Tulsa. Having submitted my presentation proposal, I was honored to be selected. My presentation title: *"How to Take the Donkey out of Training."*

The response was gratifying; we added chairs to accommodate the group. The professional trainers represented various Oklahoma-based businesses, large and small.

The room was quite warm *and* it was the first session after lunch. To add a little "strain" to the moment my handout was stapled in <u>reverse</u> order. Furthermore, another presenter's handout was mixed in at the tables. With only 45-50 minutes, I was already feeling pressure *without* the logistic challenges. Stuff happens.

The conference's keynote speaker was a well-respected trainer and "trainer of trainers." The previous afternoon, I observed his techniques as he engaged us in the pre-conference training session. Thursday morning he opened the conference and continued to demonstrate his techniques as a trainer.

Of course, that didn't influence any last minute changes of my new presentation. *I'm wiser than that!* Besides it was already pretty good; I'm not a newbie.

But my thoughts taunted me; all of these professionals were experiencing the master at work, so I'd better make some adjustments.

Yes, I tweaked my presentation early that same morning. And, yes, that meant I did not have time to rehearse my revised plan *before* presenting it.

Did I mention it was a very warm room full of professional trainers, right after lunch, with a challenging start? In fact, the room only got warmer (to me) the longer I presented. To raise the stakes higher, several companies were represented that I hoped to connect with. I know; *"Steve, what were you thinking?"*

About mid-way into the presentation, the time came to own it. When things aren't going as planned, I've learned to stop, breathe, and look at what is happening; this usually frees me to move forward. You see, I was not meeting my own expectations. But "owning it" allowed me to turn the corner and sprint to the finish.

Why do I tell you this story? This is a classic illustration of the **personal growth** principle:

> The best predictor of **future success** is the ability and willingness to learn and change achieved through **consistent reflection** on truth found in the Story.

Truth in our story comes as feedback, experience, success, and failure.

Thankfully, there were individuals who *did* connect with the message of my presentation. Their **feedback** allowed me to move forward knowing that, *in spite of myself,* I had made a difference.

What's your response to "failure"?

You can embrace "failure" as you engage in **consistent reflection**. Then, instead of "beating yourself up," you can be energized and developed by what you now recognize as truth about yourself, which leads to freedom.

Consistent reflection is about space—time, place and tools:

- **Time**: When you purposely slow down to think, review, and remember.
- **Place**: Where you go to have some uninterrupted space so you can concentrate, think, review, and remember.
- **Tools**: A journal or method to capture your thoughts, your life lessons, in order to process what's going on inside you.

Consistent reflection allows the opportunity to embrace "failure" instead of run from it into the land of insanity. That's right, where we keep doing the same thing over and over again while expecting a different result. (Thanks Albert, that's a great line!)

Our ability to grow and change hinges a lot on our willingness to learn from history, which is The Story.

> *"That men do not learn very much from the lessons of history is the most important of all the lessons of history."*
> *– Aldous Huxley*

> *"If men could learn from history, what lessons it might teach us! But passion and party blind our eyes, and the light which experience gives us is a lantern on the stern which shines only on the waves behind." – Samuel Taylor Coleridge*

> *"What experience and history teach is this - that people and governments never have learned anything from history, or acted on principles deduced from it." – G. W. F. Hegel*

"Those who cannot learn from history are doomed to repeat it." – George Santayana

To find freedom you must **create space**. Creating space is the disciplined use of time, place, and resources to reflect on the truth in your story.

What is the alternative? The loss of freedom; without creating space to reflect, we will live with limitations on our performance.

What's your hope for future success?

The hope of successful, growing people is tied to their commitment to engage in **consistent reflection**. Trust me, I've spent time reflecting on this story's feedback, experience, and my sense of failure.

Here's one of my lessons from this experience: *Challenge any assumption about last minute changes and my ability to wing it.* In fact, I may add that to the presentation. If I learn this lesson, it will take one part of the donkey out of my performance in the future. Because you know what happens when you assume, right?

Once again, I am called to listen to the "teacher" I love to hate but must embrace—**Professor Failure**.

Your future success hinges on your ability and willingness to **reflect** on the truth that comes from life. It is then that you can learn and change, and grow as a person, a manager, a leader, and a human being.

Your Personal Reflection

- ❖ How much space are you creating for reflection?

- ❖ How do you handle failure? Do you embrace it or hide from it?

- ❖ What failures from your past can you embrace as stepping stones to personal growth?

Personal Growth

The Journey of a Lifetime

~28~

The Battle for Space

Wednesday I bumped my appointment for reflection for an early morning meeting.

Thursday I bumped my appointment for reflection for something urgent: apply a second coat of stain to a table we're refinishing.

Before I knew it, another 90 minutes of my life (never to be recovered) was spent on e-mail, which lead me to read one *really important* blog after another. *Seriously?*

Not only did I misdirect the use of my time, I missed the critical personal growth opportunity that comes from daily reflection on truth found in the story, along the journey.

Transformation Takes Time

Today, you and I face forces that oppose the transformation of our lives. Three things come to my mind: *pace, distraction,* and *information overload.* Of course, there are others.

Pace: A client failed to show up for an appointment last week in large part because she has so much going on. The **pace of life** had her running hard. I even text message her the night before to confirm our meeting.

Distraction: That refinishing project took my attention away from a daily appointment set aside for personal quiet time, which is one aspect of my commitment to continuous growth. By choice, I redirected my focus.

Information Overload: Email keeps piling up and those hyperlinks lead me like a bird following a trail of grain until the snare captures my time and some portion of my life. My productivity is affected. Yes, I'm responsible, but there is that appeal to my *immediate interest* (not my **primary interest**).

Transformation is about experiencing a change in ourselves, usually an improvement. Personal growth and development takes time. The pace of life, the distractions around us, and our current information overload all seek to hinder the process of growth.

Growth is about the process of becoming more mature. We must create space—establish a time and place to tap into resources that support transformation or personal growth. We must slow down the pace to create space.

Creating space allows us to discover the truth found in our story, the story going on every day.

Information and Immediate Interest

The current level of information available to us is off the charts. What does our access to information using the internet look like?

According to the Nielsen Company, in the month of June, the average U.S. internet use in both the home and work combined includes:

- 56 sessions/visits per Person, per month
- 89 domains visited per person, per month
- 2,430 web page views per person, per month
- 56 seconds . . . the average time an American spends looking at a Web page

The statistic I find amazing is the last one: 56 seconds!

How do you think this is affecting your sense of pace and ability to process information? How is the internet affecting your practice of reflective thinking and writing required to experience transformation?

Division of Attention

What is happening to your ability to focus? To concentrate? Once again, how is the pace, the distractions and the information overload affecting your productivity, your creativity, your performance?

> *"To be everywhere is to be nowhere."*
>
> *– Seneca, Roman Philosopher*

My concern for us is that all this information is being scanned and skimmed without any *depth of reflection*. What happens when we jump from one post to another, chase one article after another riding the "Hyperlink Express"?

Have you ever spent 30 minutes reading and not have any idea, really, about what you just read?

Information without processing is like a cloud without the rain.

Nicholas Carr, best-selling author of *The Big Switch,* writes about technology's effect on the mind in his new book, *The Shallows: What the Internet is doing to our Brains.* His Saturday Essay, "Does the Internet make you Dumber?" recently appeared in the Wall Street Journal, where he noted (emphasis added):

> "...a growing body of scientific evidence suggests that the Net, with its constant **distractions and interruptions**, is also turning us into scattered and superficial thinkers.

The picture emerging from the research is deeply troubling, at least to anyone **who values the depth, rather than just the velocity, of human thought**. People who read text studded with links, the studies show, comprehend less than those who read traditional linear text. People who watch busy multimedia presentations remember less than those who take in information in a more sedate and focused manner. People who are continually distracted by emails, alerts and other messages understand less than those who are **able to concentrate**. And people who juggle many tasks are **less creative and less productive** than those who do one thing at a time.

The common thread in these disabilities is **the division of attention**.

What we seem to be sacrificing in all our surfing and searching is our **capacity to engage** in the quieter, **attentive modes of thought** that underpin contemplation, reflection and introspection. *The Web never encourages us to slow down.* It keeps us in a state of perpetual mental locomotion.

It is revealing, and distressing, to compare the cognitive effects of the Internet with those of an earlier information technology, the printed book. Whereas the Internet scatters our attention, the book focuses it. Unlike the screen, the page promotes contemplativeness.

Reading a long sequence of pages helps us develop a rare kind of mental discipline. *The innate bias of the human brain, after all, is to be distracted.* Our predisposition is to be aware of as much of what's going on around us as possible. Our fast-paced, reflexive shifts in focus were once crucial to our survival. They reduced the odds that a predator would take us by surprise or that we'd overlook a nearby source of food.

To read a book is to practice *an unnatural process of thought.* It requires us to place ourselves at what T. S. Eliot, in his poem "Four Quartets," called "the still point of the turning world." We have to forge or strengthen the neural links needed to counter our *instinctive distractedness,* thereby *gaining greater control over our attention and our mind.*

It is this control, this mental discipline that we are at risk of losing as we spend ever more time scanning and skimming online. If the slow progression of words across printed pages damped our craving to be inundated by mental stimulation, the Internet indulges it. It returns us to our **native state of distractedness**, while presenting us with far more distractions than our ancestors ever had to contend with."

As an executive coach, I am privileged to support my clients' efforts to create space for reflective thinking and writing. The result? Transformation, changed behavior, improved performance, and increased results.

To create space requires us to take control of the pace, minimize the distractions, and limit the information flow. Creating space for personal growth is about setting aside time, having a place, and tapping into supportive resources. Resources can include books, great questions, a mentor, a coach, a friend; the story with feedback, experience, success, or failure.

As you've read before, the best predictor of sustainable success is your ability and willingness to learn and change achieved through consistent reflection on the story for truth. This is the disciplined approach to life that will reward you with amazing transformation and improved performance.

Your Personal Reflection

❖ What in your life is holding you back from achieving personal growth?

❖ Based on the reality of "The Battle for Personal Development," what steps are you taking to create space for reflective thinking?

❖ How are you managing the pace, distraction, and overload potential of our day and technology?

ࣾ20ࣹ

The Low Cost of Growth

It arrived in the morning mail. The envelope was stamped:

"It doesn't cost much to leave it all behind."

Jim Berra's letter addresses one of my life's challenges—finding the perfect vacation. He then offers an alternative—ditch the stress and head straight for fun—and suggests an easy and value-driven action—book now and save up to 20%.

You guessed it, a sales proposal for a Caribbean cruise. *"It doesn't cost much to leave it all behind."*

As a certified executive coach, I see nearly everything in relationship to our growth as people; the cruise "invitation" is no exception.

What could you "leave behind"?

One of the coaching exercises I love to use is adapted from Marshall Goldsmith's work. It lists 21 of the common challenges leaders face in *interpersonal and leadership behavior*. The assignment is to identify your top three from the list.

Leadership development is often positioned as gaining a new skill. Sure that is part of it. But maturity as a leader is not always about what you must start doing. Sometimes the solution is simply to **stop** that limiting behavior.

For example, one of the 21 limiting behaviors is *"winning too much."* This is a need to win at all costs and in all situations—whether it matters or not.

Not you? How about this one: *"claiming credit that you don't deserve,"*—that inclination and annoying overestimation of your contribution.

Here's good news: it doesn't cost much to leave these limiting behaviors behind.

However, what's *that* costing you?

While the cruise invitation suggests it doesn't cost **much** to leave it all behind, there is a cost.

To stop a leadership-limiting, interpersonal behavior, the first step is to **notice**. Consistently reflecting on how we show up and to seek feedback allows us to start noticing. Reflection requires we create space – have time and a place to record our observations. A journal can be helpful.

With increased awareness and simple honesty you can tap into your support system for accountability, add a reminder, and make the decision to stop.

What's the upside?

Consider the ripple effects:

- Others will appreciate your honesty
- You will earn greater respect
- Increased respect enhances trust
- Trust is a critical to leadership effectiveness

The cost of growth verses the cost of ignoring limiting behavior indicates *"it doesn't cost much to leave it all behind."*

Your Personal Reflection

- ❖ What core people-skill behavior challenges are limiting your influence?

- ❖ What is that unproductive leadership behavior costing you?

- ❖ How might you go about changing this behavior?

৯30৩

What's Your Pain Tolerance?

Growing pains are often experienced by children and teenagers supposedly when they are growing fast. According to the Mayo Clinic website (emphasis added):

> "Growing pains tend to affect both legs and occur at night. In many instances, growing pains will wake a child from sleep. The term "growing pains" may be a misnomer because there's **no evidence that growth hurts**."

While there may be "no evidence that growth hurts" in the physical development of children, what about in the personal development of people?

How does pain help?

Pain increases our desire to learn and change—to embrace growth opportunities.

Recently, I was learned the story of one of my executive coaching clients and what brought him to the coaching engagement and this new chapter in his journey.

He sold his company and was now in the midst of a major transition after a successful career of 30 years. We were listening to the story for truth. It was revealing when he said, "I didn't hurt enough, so I didn't make the changes 5-6 years ago."

This is not an indictment or judgment. It is a fact: **personal growth is often hindered due to our *high tolerance for pain*.** No, I'm not talking about physical pain.

If you were on a hike, how long would you tolerate a small pebble in your boot?

If you are hurt by someone, how long would you tolerate the anger, bitterness, resentment, and negative health impact associated with holding a grudge?

What's the difference?

The pain is present and a solution is available. Most of us stop as soon as we feel the pain of the pebble. Then, there is this matter of taking offense. How long do you tolerate the pain before tapping into the solution and offer forgiveness?

Yes, there are other contributing factors to our resistance. As people, we seem to fit into one of three positions regarding a behavior change:

1. We know something is holding us back, but we're just **too busy** to deal with it.
2. We know something is getting in our way, but **don't know what to do.**
3. We don't realize we are limiting ourselves, but everyone else does; it's **a blind spot.**

People committed to personal growth and success notice unproductive behavior and initiate change, which improves their performance. It's a powerful response. Influence and credibility increase as others observe real, sustained changes in behavior.

Pain Tolerance Exposed—It's Painful

As an executive coach, I build trust, ask questions, and provide objectivity to support the growth effort. This can be uncomfortable, if not downright painful. The desired outcome—improved performance and expanded personal influence—brings a positive impact on life and business. It's awesome—the pebble is out of the boot!

Opposition to change (personal growth) stands in resistance *until* our pain pushes us to break through **the wall of resistance**.

What holds you back from tapping into your ability to learn and change when there is not enough pain to push you through the resistance?

What is "enough pain"?

If your pain tolerance is high, it will take more pain to jolt you into action. In other words, a high pain tolerance hinders our ability and willingness to learn and grow as people.

When the pain invites us to pay attention to the story, we can embrace the truth. We have a choice; we can:

1. **Manage the pain**, which often leads to unintended consequences.
2. **Embrace the pain**, which usually removes our resistance to change and leads to improved performance and enjoyment of life

No pain, no change. No change, no gain.

Pain as emotional or mental distress is a gift designed to help us stop, take stock, and engage the process of growth. And it's never too late to engage the process of growth.

Your Personal Reflection

❖ Consider this: on a scale of 1 to 6 (1 = very low; 6 = extremely high) what is your pain tolerance? If it is high, how is this affecting your willingness to change? What is that costing you?

❖ Where are you feeling pain in your life today? What needs to change?

❖ What support do you need to make that change?

❧31❧

Four-D Change

Change.

Perhaps you have heard the often-repeated quote of Henry David Thoreau regarding change.

"Things do not change; we change."

A rather effective leader in the fight for equal rights for everyone was King Whitney, Jr., who wrote:

> "Change has a considerable psychological impact on the human mind. To the fearful it is threatening because it means that things may get worse. To the hopeful it is encouraging because things may get better. To the confident it is inspiring because the challenge exists to make things better."

Change seems to be one of those things people tend to love or hate. Perhaps it's because:

- Our response depends on the source of the suggested change—"their" idea vs. "my" idea
- It depends on how much we care about whatever is being "left behind"
- It depends on how we think about change

I invite you to take a minute with the following questions:

What one thing would you like to change?

Where would a change in your life bring you greater freedom, peace, joy, success, influence, results . . . ?

Go ahead; name it. The more precise the better.

Which of the following best describes your thinking about this journey of change: fearful, hopeful, or confident?

Dig a little deeper. If . . .

- **Fearful** – What is creating this fear within you about making that specific change?
- **Hopeful** – How does the thought of making that change encourage you?
- **Confident** – What gives you faith to believe the best is yet to be, once you make the change?

The change I'm asking you to think about is within your authority to bring about; it is about your life. Making the change will release you to greater success and influence—change within your thinking, behavior, and performance.

How do you move from here to there?

Here are four steps associated with *The Journey of Change.*

1. **Desire.** This is more than a simple wish; it is a longing, craving, or yearning. Think chocolate. **Desire is where it begins.**

    What if we lack the desire to make this change? Get ready for **desperation**. Only when desperation (pain) exceeds resistance will we move forward, laying aside something "old" for something "new." Are you desperate, yet? Can you imagine the consequences if you don't make this change?

Desire fueled by desperation becomes enhanced with understanding. When we **comprehend the benefits** of making a change, our desire to make the change will increase. Can you imagine the reward when you make this change?

Desire is where change starts. Desperation and understanding help develop an action-oriented desire.

2. **Discipline.** What comes to your mind with the word "discipline"? In this context, discipline is about "doing"; a systematic method to getting something done. With adequate desire to make a "change" we must take action, discipline gives us a path or framework for victory.

   Often what we need is a **commitment to consistency** to achieve the desired outcome. What must you do to arrive at your goal? What action is so doable it is laughable; meaning your response to the action step is: "I can do that!" Desire leads to doing.

3. **Determination.** Significant change in behavior must be supported by determination. Opposition is part of the journey. Old habits, old ways of thinking, comfort zones, fears, doubt, and natural resistance rise up to defeat *The Journey of Change*. Our commitment of will and clarity on why supports the resolve to see it through.

4. **Delight.** The personal development *Journey of Change* begins with some level of desperation and understanding; we recognize the need. **Desire moves us to Doing; Doing**

is supported by Determination - until the new behavior **becomes a delight.**

Positive change brings its own reward, which includes enjoyment and pleasure (imagine eating chocolate or one of your other favorite candies). *The Journey of Change* moves us from fear and resistance *to* accomplishment and delight including the positive rewards of growth!

Your Personal Reflection

❖ Where are you on the Journey of Change?

❖ Which do you need? Desire, discipline, or determination?

❖ What change have you made in the past that brings you delight today?

ಇ32ಏ

Is it Selfish?

As our coaching conversation continued, Susan recounted several stories from the past week, both professionally and personally, indicating the significant growth she is experiencing. She works in Human Resources as a corporate trainer.

She is investing in her own personal growth as an emerging leader.

Recently, her manager (unannounced) sat in on one of her training sessions.

In the recent past, she would have reacted; this time she responded. How did she respond?

- She **noticed** her emotions, took a deep breath, and examined her thinking.
- This allowed her to **stop** the emotional reaction.
- This also **silenced** the assumptive voices playing with her head.
- This allowed her to take a minute to **examine** her thinking and **change it.**
- She received positive **feedback** from her boss for her **improved performance.**

We celebrated!

After sharing a couple of other real-world incidents, a puzzled look came over her face; she was processing. "I don't understand how all this focus on me fits with serving others as a leader. It seems a little *selfish* to give all this attention to me."

Starting with the obvious, I ask, "Are you a woman, wife, and mother?" Pause. "What is it you normally do in all your roles?"

"Nurture others, take care of them . . ." The light went on.

"What do you see happening in your relationships . . . with your boss, your co-worker, even your husband as a result of this effort on you developing you?" (Her stories from the previous week had involved each of these individuals.)

"Things are better," she observed.

"Indeed, your influence is increasing, and if leadership is influence, then giving attention to your own development has increased your leadership, improved your performance, and the ramifications on others are positive, right?"

Indeed, one benefit of being an "unselfish leader" through giving attention to your personal development is the benefit to others. In addition, you also get to enjoy your improved performance.

Dr. Marshall Goldsmith, author of 26 books, including What Got You Here Won't Get You There, a New York Times best-seller and Wall Street Journal #1 business book, tells about General Mills CEO Steve Sanger in this Fast Company article *"To Develop Others, Start with Yourself."* Here are some excerpts (emphasis added):

> "Listen to what General Mills CEO Steve Sanger recently told 90 of his colleagues: "As you all know, last year my team told me that I needed to do a better job of coaching my direct reports...I have been working on becoming a better coach for the past year or so. I'm still not doing quite

as well as I want, but I'm getting a lot better. My coworkers have been helping me improve."

While listening to Steve speak ... I realized how much the world has changed. Twenty years ago, few CEOs received feedback from their colleagues [or] discussed their personal developmental plans. Today, many of the world's most respected chief executives are setting a positive example by opening up, striving continually to **develop themselves as leaders**. In fact, organizations that do the best job of cranking out leaders tend to have CEOs like Steve Sanger who are directly and actively involved in leadership development.

No question, **one of the best ways** top executives can get their leaders to improve is **to work on improving themselves**. Leading by example can mean a lot more than leading by public-relations hype.

Unfortunately, CEO **arrogance can have the opposite effect**. When the boss acts like a little god and tells everyone else they need to improve, that behavior can be copied at every level of management. *Every level then points out how the level **below** it needs to change.* The result: No one gets much better.

The principle of leadership development by personal example doesn't apply just to CEOs. It applies to all levels of management. ***All good leaders want their people to grow and develop on the job.*** Who knows? ***If we work hard to improve ourselves, we might even encourage the people around us to do the same thing.***"

Yes, we celebrated Susan's personal growth and performance improvement.

As she closed her journal, she ran her fingers over the title of her coaching resource, *Next Level Journal . . . Accelerated Personal Development.* She now understands the concept of *accelerated* personal development.

Susan's relationships are stronger, her influence is growing, and her performance is improving. Her stress is lower, life is better; *very worthwhile wouldn't you say?*

> *"Great leaders encourage leadership development by openly developing themselves."*
> – Marshall Goldsmith

Your Personal Reflection:

❖ What are your thoughts on the need to develop yourself as a leader?

❖ How are you openly developing yourself?

❖ What do you think is your biggest hindrance to intentional personal growth?

๛33๛

Breaking Personal Growth Barriers

Breaking the sound barrier with an aircraft provides a stunning sight and sound. This accelerated speed, which exceeds the speed of sound, is often achieved by our military aircraft.

Here is a technical description of this moment:

> "The passage from subsonic to supersonic speeds is accompanied by some unusual phenomena which lie in the realm of "nonlinear" mechanical events - events involving some degree of chaos."

The first man credited with breaking the sound barrier in level flight is Chuck Yeager. He did so in October 1947, while flying at an altitude of 45,000 feet.

The Personal Growth Barrier

A barrier is something that obstructs or limits.

In terms of personal growth, our behavior is the observable manifestation of a "growth barrier"—something that limits or obstructs sustained or future success.

In simple terms, success is simply the achievement of something; doing what you set out to do.

Success is defined *by you for you*; based on your **values**, your **purpose** in life, and your **passion**. This is a place of great freedom.

A barrier, in terms of personal growth, is something that limits your ability to achieve what you set out to accomplish in life with your life. It is most often displayed in so-called "soft skills" or people skills—the relational side of life not the technical. Again, this shows up as unproductive, limiting behavior . . . a barrier.

When do you know there is a barrier?

Look again at the technical description of breaking the sound barrier: ". . . events involving some degree of chaos."

Where there is turmoil, confusion, frustration, poor performance, or unproductive activity pay attention. Observe it and you'll find the barrier to your success.

Watch for fear-based emotion (worry, anxiety, anger, hate, rate, hostility, ill-will, resentment, frustration, impatience, irritation, bitterness). Such fear-based emotion triggers **ancient behavior**, such as:

- Micro-managing
- Obsessive control
- Lack of delegation
- Procrastination
- Poor decision making
- Ineffective communication
- Telling
- Poor listening
- Lack of trust
- Assumptions

These old behaviors are a barrier hindering your full potential and future success.

Let's now take a look at what hampers our ability to accelerate our personal growth:

> **Blame** – Placing the responsibility on someone else.

> **Denial** – Refusing to acknowledge the truth/reality.

> **Rationalization** – Making excuses, avoiding responsibility for your performance.

> **Minimization** – Underestimating intentionally; "It's no big deal."

> **Avoidance** – Withdrawing from or avoiding the reality of the situation.

How do you break a personal growth barrier?

My executive coaching process is not hard; it's just not easy—at least not without support. Objectivity also helps.

Here are four steps to breaking a performance barrier:

1. **Acknowledge.** What is getting in your way?
2. **Observe.** When does the behavior happen?
3. **Change.** What is your preferred response?
4. **Evaluate.** How will I know I made the change?

The critical skill and practical habit that supports sustained success is consistent reflection.

> *The best predictor of continued success is the ability and willingness to learn and change achieved through* ***consistent reflection*** *on truth found in the story.*

The reality for all of us is this . . .

> What got you here (your current level of success),
> will not get you there (your next level of success);
> whether its job performance or in life . . .
> mentally, physically, emotionally, or spiritually.

Your Personal Reflection

❖   What is your growth barrier?

❖   What seems to be hindering your future success?

❖   What steps are you taking to create space for reflective thinking and behavior change?

❧34❧

What If . . . ?

Part of the inspiration for this lesson came from a source that I'll admit to later. But first things first.

Power provides us the ability, strength, and capacity to do something. We previously explored how questions have power. However, **open-ended** questions are really *a request for information and designed to help us stop and explore for truth.*

> Questions help us give **careful thought to reality** . . . the **facts**, when examined, become feedback. **Truth allows us to choose**; we can change unproductive behavior, enlarge our influence (leadership), and achieve success . . . yes, make a difference in the world.

Reflecting on life with questions gives us an ability, strength and capacity to change unproductive behavior(s), improve our performance, and make a difference in our world. That's power!

In like fashion, there are two little words that have power, especially when combined. They are **what** and **if**.

This obvious connection came back to me recently, as my wife Rita and I watched the movie *Letters to Juliet*. Yes, I know. It's a "chick-flick," a romantic film with a predictable, yet engaging, story line. Nevertheless, I enjoyed the movie.

The film is the story of one letter written to the fictional Juliet Montague of Shakespeare's play that is answered 50 years after it was written and what happens when the founder of the letter replies.

The film creates space with empty dirt roads, architecture, food, sidewalk cafés, and cobblestone streets found in Italy. It seems like a very romantic place.

> "In Verona, Italy – the beautiful city where Romeo first met Juliet – there is a place where the heartbroken leave notes asking Juliet for her help. It's there that aspiring writer Sophie finds a 50-year-old letter that will change her life forever. As she sets off on a romantic journey of the heart with the letter's author, Claire, now a grandmother, and her handsome grandson, all three will discover that sometimes the greatest love story ever told is your own."

Come on, who couldn't use a little romance?

At one point, Claire reads the letter Sophie wrote that started the search for Lorenzo:

> ""What" and "if" are two words as non-threatening as words can be; but put them together side by side and they have the power to haunt you for the rest of your life.
> What if?
> What if?
> I don't know how your story ended but if it was true love back then, it is never too late. If it was true love then, why wouldn't it be now? You need only the courage to follow your heart."

Yes, this is about your personal growth and leadership journey. It is about that dream that still flickers. It is about the decision you wait to make while postponing the adventure, the solution, the thrill of making a difference in someone's life, or even the world.

"What if" can haunt us or set us on an adventure or journey of a lifetime.

My perspective on the story of life is simple:

- **Everyone** has a story.
- Every day you **add to** your story.
- Today, you will **have influence** on someone's story.

What if...

> You make that call?
> Write that letter?
> Apply for that open position?
> Forgive the offender?
> Take the risk?
> Start your own business?
> Take that class? Teach that group?
> Mentor that person, ask to be mentored?
> What if you care or love?
> What if you act on your plan to get out of debt?
> What if you read one book a month?
> What if you change your eating and exercise habits?
> What if you change your thinking about . . . ?

What if . . . ?

It won't spoil the movie to let you know what you already know. Claire and Lorenzo had lived 50 years of their journey when Claire answered the question: What if Lorenzo is still alive?

Remember, **power** provides us the ability, strength, and capacity to do something; to take action.

A question is simply "a request for information, when properly framed, that helps you **stop and explore** for truth." The power of a question comes from the truthfulness of the answer.

Truth Brings Freedom

What do we need to move forward? Truth, facts, and reality. Without truth we remain stuck in fear.

The power of a question is how it helps us to stop and think.

When we give careful thought or *reconsider previous actions, events, or decisions,* we find the path to freedom. Feedback is that factual, truthful answer; when embraced, it can set us free to experience even greater success.

Reflecting on "the story" using open-ended questions provides us with the ability, strength, and capacity to:

- Change unproductive behavior(s)
- Improve performance
- Make a difference in our world.

Now, that's power!

The Big Picture

Asking "What if?" can give us the power to take a risk and set us on the adventure of a lifetime. Consider Pablo Picasso's perspective on risk-taking:

> *"I am always doing that which I cannot do, in order that I may learn how to do it."*

The use of "What if?" sets us free to explore potential, which usually involves some level of risk.

*"This nation was built by men who took risks - pioneers who were **not afraid** of the wilderness, business men who were **not afraid** of failure, scientists who were **not afraid** of the truth, thinkers who were **not afraid** of progress, dreamers who were **not afraid** of action."*

– Brooks Atkinson

What if . . . ?

Asking yourself this powerful little question just might lead to a personal breakthrough.

Your Personal Reflection

❖ Do you desire power to invite your risk-taker to "show up" and take action?

❖ Do you want power to tell that procrastinator to "get lost" and take action?

❖ What might happen when you ask "What if?" when . . .

  • You feel inclined to hit the **snooze button**?
  • You want to click the **postpone button** on the task reminder once again?
  • You are prompted to reach out to another person offering positive support?

Conclusion

☙Conclusion☙

Mountain Climbers Don't Climb Alone

Outward Bound was a fantastic part of my Executive Leadership Program that I enjoyed when I worked for Atlanta-based Cox Enterprises a few years ago. The executive leadership expedition took our group to North Carolina and Pisgah National Forest.

Here's how the Outward Bound literature sums things up:

> "Embrace the challenge. Go beyond the expected. Learn through experience. Realize the potential ... for yourself and a better world. Challenge yourself. Change your world. Outward Bound."

Our four-day wilderness adventure presented me the opportunity to do things I had never done before. In addition to several days of backpacking, I experienced my first rappelling and rock climbing adventure.

During the course of our expedition, we received on-the-spot leadership lessons while planning and executing a real-time mountaineering expedition. Everything from inclement weather to group dynamics impacted and directed the challenges we faced.

We shared responsibility for the leadership and communication dynamics of our team along with the guides, safety officers, and mentors. The expedition was a significant source of learning and discovery.

No question, the challenging experience impacted my life and leadership.

One of the gifts I returned home with is what I call "Lessons from the Forest." Here are five basic principles:

1. The Foundation of Trust
2. The Necessity of Risk
3. The Power of Focus
4. The Strength of Teamwork
5. The Simplicity of Life

The Next Level Journey is about growth and "the opportunity to do things" you've never done before. The preparation, the challenge, the experience, the victory are all part of my story, now.

Edmund Hillary, the New Zealander mountain climber famous for being the first to climb Mount Everest is reported to have said, *"It is not the mountain we conquer but ourselves."*

What does it take for you to achieve your next level in life?

Mountain climbers don't climb alone. Everyone needs help and encouragement; in a word, **support**. The greater our challenge is the greater the need for support.

In mountaineering, support is about securing the climber's rope. To belay the climber, his rope is fastened or controlled by wrapping it around a metal device or another person. This provides support for the climber to take greater risk in his climb or descent. Trust is critical to the relationship. Together the teamwork allows the climber to focus on his climb knowing he is supported.

Who is your belay?

In coaching, one of my exercises is focused on my client's "Support System." We explore three levels of support:

1. What do you do for you that can do by yourself to support your well-being?
2. Who is in your inner circle, people who understand you, who ask tough questions all while believing in you?
3. What else is in your world charges your batteries and supports your commitment to growth?

There is a lot of life going on these days. So whether you think of this in terms of your next level at work, in your career, on that big project, or in everyday life support is critical to your success.

Keeping in mind that mountain climbers don't climb alone—how are you supporting your personal development journey?

About the Author

❧About the Author❦

Steve Laswell

"The business of business is people. The ability to influence people is a core skill of today's leader."

Steve is the founder of Next level Executive Coaching, LLC and author of *The Journey: Personal Notes from the Father*. With a passion for helping people reach their full potential, he is one of the most effective certified executive coaches in America.

With a client base that spans across the nation, Steve helps people reap the benefits of creating space for reflective thinking and writing as a way to support lasting *behavior change* and *improved performance*.

From Fortune 500 companies to privately held businesses, Steve coaches a wide range of professionals, including C-level executives, vice presidents, managers, physicians, pastors, business owners, and entrepreneurs across a variety of industries.

Steve's diverse experience, empowering perspective, and natural talents come from his 20 years of pastoral ministry, 10 years of business experience in radio, and 5-year journey as an entrepreneur and small business owner.

Steve earned his TCU Sherpa Coach certification through The Neeley School of Business. He also has a Master's Degree from Southern Nazarene University, Bethany, Oklahoma. He is a member of the International Coach Federation and the American Society of Training Development. Steve is also very active in his community and church.

For over 35 years, Steve has made the journey with his best friend and wife Rita. Together, they have three amazing daughters and sons-in-law, who have given them nine grandchildren.

Steve enjoys spending time outdoors, cooking on his grill, and enjoying his Japanese Kio pond. As an amateur photographer, he has fun expressing his creativity while capturing memories of the journey.

Take the Next Step

After reading *The People Project*, take the next step and engage Steve Laswell. His effective 1on1 and group coaching services are of great value to personal, leadership, and employee development programs.

To have Steve personally address your organization or to retain his services for your own personal journey, please contact him at:

Email: steve@NextLevelExecutiveCoaching.com
Phone: (918) 296-7785

To learn more about Steve and how others have benefited from his coaching services, visit **www.NextLevelExecutiveCoaching.com.**

Sources

∽Sources∾

Ch 1

1.	National Geographic. "Porcupine." *National Geographic.* Web. 8 April 2011 http://animals.nationalgeographic.com/animals/mammals/porcupine/

Ch 4

1.	Carson, Ben M.D. (1990). *Gifted Hands.* Review and Herald Publishing Association. Amazon Book Review. Web. 8 April 2011 http://books.google.com/books?id=iW_dw1Qh_BQC&pg=PT100&lpg=PT100&dq=What+page?+In+any+career,+whether+it's+that+of+a+TV+repairman,+a+musician,+a+secretary+-+or+a+surgeon+-+an+individual+must+believe+in+himself+and+in+his+abilities.&source=bl&ots=gCt3dxeDcO&sig=1as2S5VpW05xr32sXkFfajq9LSU&hl=en&ei=O2WfTcn8DeTw0gGfqfSdBQ&sa=X&oi=book_result&ct=result&resnum=1&ved=0CBQQ6AEwAA#v=onepage&q&f=false

Ch 5

1.	Bregman, Peter. "Why Friends Matter at Work and in Life." Harvard Business Review, July 1, 2010. Web. 8 April 2011 http://blogs.hbr.org/bregman/2010/07/why-friends-matter-at-work-and.html

Ch 7

1.	Covey, Stephen R. "The 4 Steps to Finding Your Voice." Stephen R. Covey, April 24, 2008. Web. 8 April 2011 http://www.stephencovey.com/blog/?p=16

2.	"Gallup Publishes Long-Awaited Follow-Up to Bestselling Management book." Gallup Management Journal, November 8, 2006. Web. 8 April 2011 http://gmj.gallup.com/content/25390/Gallup-Publishes-Long-Awaited-Follow-Up-to.aspx

Ch. 8
1.   "The High Cost of Disengaged Employees." Gallup
Management Journal, April 15, 2002. Web. 8 April 2011
http://gmj.gallup.com/ content/247/high-cost-disengaged-
employees.aspx

2.   Sulkowicz, Kerry. "CEOs at Citigroup: Authenticity
Desperately Needed." BNET, March 3, 2010. Web. 8 April 2011
http://www.bnet.com/blog/business-psychology/ceos-at-
citigroup-authenticity-desperately-needed/132

Ch 9
1.   "5 Keys to Engagement." Closing the Engagement Gap. Web.
8 April 2011 http://www.towersperrin.com/gap/keys.htm

Ch 10
1.   Conseil, Dominique. "Aveda Mission." Aveda. Web. 8 April
2011 http://www.aveda.com/aboutaveda/mission.tmpl

Ch 11
1.   "Life Rules." Games Information Depot. Web. 8 April 2011
http://www.gamesinfodepot.com/games/board/life/rules/

2.   Merriam-Webster, "game." Merriam-Webster. Web. 8 April
2011 http://www.merriam-webster.com/dictionary/game

Ch. 13
1.   Stovall, Jim. Ultimate Productivity. Nashville, TN: Thomas
Nelson, 2008. Print.

Ch 14
1.   Amabile, Teresa M., and Steven J. Kramer. "The HBR List:
Breakthrough Ideas for 2010: 1. What Really Motivates Workers."
Harvard Business Review. Web. 8 April 2011 http://hbr.org/2010/
01/the-hbr-list-breakthrough-ideas-for-2010/ar/1

Ch. 16

1. "The Fastest Pitcher in Baseball History," Baseball Almanac, February 2003. Web. 8 April 2011 http://www.baseball-almanac.com/articles/fastest-pitcher-in-baseball.shtml

Ch. 17

1. Ayers, Keith. *Engagement is Not Enough.* Charleston, SC: Advantage Media Group, 2009. Print.

Ch. 18

1. The Thompson Chain-Reference Bible – NIV. Grand Rapids, MI: Zondervan Bible Publishers. p. 660. Print.

2. Wikipedia. "Prudence." Wikipedia. Web. 8 April 2011 http://en.wikipedia.org/wiki/Prudence

Ch. 19

1. IMDb. "Memorable quotes for Jaws (1975)." IMDb. Web. 8 April 2011 http://www.imdb.com/title/tt0073195/quotes

2. Wikipedia. "Occupational Safety and Health Administration." Wikipedia. Web. 8 April 2011 http://en.wikipedia.org/wiki/Occupational_Safety_and_Health_Administration

Ch. 20

1. Ferriss, Tim. "The Truth – Stats & Research." The Blog of Tim Ferriss. Web. 8 April 2011 http://www.fourhourworkweek.com/blog/the-truth/#top

2. Main, Frank. "Cop seeks OT for blackberry use." *Chicago Sun-Times*, July 31, 2010. Web. 8 April 2011 http://nl.newsbank.com/nl-search/we/Archives?p_product=CSTB&p_theme=cstb&p_action=search&p_maxdocs=200&s_dispstring=rest(Jeffrey%20Allen%20)%20AND%20date(all)&p

_field_advanced-0=&p_text_advanced-0=("Jeffrey%20Allen%20")&
xcalnumdocs=20&p_perpage=10&p_sort=YMD_date:D&xcal_usewe
ights=no

3.   "Millennials, A Portrait of Generation Next." Pew Research
Center, February 2010. Web. 8 April 2011
http://pewsocialtrends.org/files/2010/10/millennials-confident-
connected-open-to-change.pdf

4.   Freeburn, Christopher. "Feeling overworked? How to beat
small business burnout." Small Business Online Community, July
29, 2010. Web. 8 April 2011 http://smallbusinessonlinecommunity
.bankofamerica.com/blogs/GeneralBusiness/2010/07/29/feeling-
overworked-how-to-beat-small-business-burnout

Ch 21
1.   Grace, Roger M. "At 10-2 and 4 O'clock, It was Dr. Pepper
Time." *Metropolitan News-Enterprise*, December 15, 2005. Web. 8
April 2011 http://www.metnews.com/articles/2005/
reminiscing121505.htm

Ch 22
1.   Wikipedia. "Work-life Balance." Wikipedia. Web. 8 April
2011 http://en.wikipedia.org/wiki/Work%E2%80%93life balance

Ch. 23
1.   "2009 Corporate Citizenship Report." Texas Instruments.
Web. 8 April 2011 http://www.ti.com/corp/docs/csr/
empwellbeing/worklife/rentention.shtml#top

2.   CareerBuilder. "CareerBuilder Research Indentifies Signs
You Just May be a Workaholic." CareerBuilder, December 15, 2010.
Web. 8 April 2011 http://www.careerbuilder.com/share/aboutus/
pressreleasesdetail.aspx?id=pr610&sd=12%2f17%2f2010&ed=12
%2f31%2f2010&siteid=cbpr&sc_cmp1=cb_pr610

3.   Stock, Kyle. "New Model for Work-Life Balance on Wall Street?" *The Wall Street Journal*, January 3, 2011. Web. 8 April 2011 http://blogs.wsj.com/juggle/2011/01/03/the-jungle-new-model-for-work-life-balance-on-wall-street/?KEYWORDS=work+life+balance

Ch. 24
1.   Bregman, Peter. "Why I Returned My iPad." *Harvard Business Review*, June 16, 2010. Web. 8 April 2011 http://blogs.hbr.org/bregman/2010/06/why-i-returned-my-ipad.html

Ch. 28
1.   "June 2010: Top Online Sites and Brands in U. S." The Nielsen Company, July 16, 2010. Web. 8 April 2011. http://blog.nielsen.com/nielsenwire/online_mobile/june-2010-top-online-sites-and-brands-in-the-u-s

2.   Carr, Nicholas. "Does the Internet Make You Dumber?" *The Wall Street Journal*. The Saturday Essay, June 5, 2010. Web. 8 April 2011 http://online.wsj.com/article/SB10001424052748704025304575284981644790098.html

Ch. 30
1.   Mayo Clinic Staff. "Growing Pains." Mayo Clinic, November 16, 2010. Web. 8 April 2011 http://www.mayoclinic.com/health/growing-pains/DS00888

Ch. 32
1.   Goldsmith, Marshall. "To Help Others Develop, Start with Yourself." Fast Company, March 1, 2004. Web. 8 April 2011 http://www.fastcompany.com/magazine/80/mgoldsmith.html

Ch. 33
   1.   "Breaking the Sound Barrier with an Aircraft."
Hyperphysics. Web. 8 April 2011 http://hyperphysics.phy-astr.gsu.edu/hbase/sound/soubar.html

Ch 34
   1.   *Letters to Juliet* (2010). Letters to Juliet. Web. 8 April 2011 http://www.letterstojuliet-movie.com

Made in the USA
San Bernardino, CA
24 April 2015